CHIPLOQUORGAN;

OR,

LIFE BY THE CAMP FIRE

IN

DOMINION OF CANADA AND NEWFOUNDLAND.

BY

RICHARD LEWES DASHWOOD,

XV. REGIMENT.

New Edition.

LONDON:

SIMPKIN, MARSHALL & CO.

4 STATIONERS' HALL COURT.

1872.

CHIPLOQUORGAN.

Camp near Pleasant Brook, New Brunswick.

PREFACE.

THE word " Chiploquorgan " is the Indian name,
in the Milicite language, for the stick on which
the kettle is suspended over the camp fire, as
depicted on the cover of this book. The Indians
attach a certain degree of superstition to the
Chiploquorgan, and it is considered most unlucky to burn or remove it on leaving a camp.

CHIPLOQUORGAN.

CHAPTER I.

Sail for North America—Mishaps on the Voyage—Arrival at St. John,
New Brunswick—First impressions of the town—My first fishing
expedition—American Hotels—The Schoodic Lakes—Yankee
"Sportsmen"—Trout fishing—The Schoodic Indians—The
musquitoes, and how to get rid of them.

On the 24th of January, 1862, I sailed in the
steam transport Adelaide, from Cork, for North
America, with six companies of my regiment,
which formed part of the force sent from England at that time, in consequence of the seizure
by an American man-of-war of Messrs. Mason
and Slidell, while passengers on board the royal
mail steamer Trent.

After our engines breaking down on several
occasions, and meeting other damages from a

1

severe hurricane, we were obliged to put back to Plymouth for repairs. Here we were detained three weeks; and at the end of that time we sailed for St. John, New Brunswick. We were ordered to take the southern route as a means of avoiding the rough storms of the North Atlantic, against which our ship had proved herself totally unequal to make any headway. We were also ordered to touch at the Bermudas for coals. We reached those islands with just enough coal to take us into port. We stayed there ten days, and eventually reached St. John, New Brunswick, on the 24th of March, seventy-nine days after our original departure from Cork. If we had embarked in one of Cunard's or Inman's steamers, we should probably have crossed the Atlantic in a fortnight, and besides having a pleasanter voyage, the saving of expense would have been considerable.

The Adelaide was quite unfit to cross the Atlantic at that time of year, her engines being deficient in power, and being moreover old-fashioned and worn-out. Their defective state may be imagined from the fact that they broke down altogether about ten times.

The Victoria, the sister ship of the Adelaide, sailed from Cork with the 96th regiment on board, the day after we·left that port.   She proved even in a worse state than the Adelaide, for besides being defective in her engines, her rigging was rotten.   She also put back to refit, and starting again for America, got no farther than the Azores (she was likewise ordered to take the southern route), when her engines breaking down, she was obliged to return to port; nor did she make another attempt to cross the "herring pond."   It is to be hoped that the lives of British soldiers will never again be entrusted to either of these ill-fated vessels.

I had always a great longing to be quartered in North America, and make practical acquaintance with the various sports to be obtained in that country.   My keenness had also been much increased by the description given to me by a near relative, who, thirty years ago, was quartered in New Brunswick with the 34th regiment, and who spent all his leave in the woods.   The Indians at Fredericton, to this day, speak of him as a well-remembered sportsman of the right sort, or, as an old Indian said one day when referring

to him, " He great hunter, good hand in woods,
same as Indian in canoe."

On disembarking at St. John I was much
struck with the appearance of the town, which
was both novel and interesting: the sleighs flying about in all directions; little boys sliding
down the hilly streets on small hand-sleighs, and
gliding just clear of the horses when a collision
appeared certain.   This amusement is called
"coasting;" and in winter appears to take the
place of the marbles and peg-top of the boys at
home.   Having shaken down into barracks, I
began to make inquiries as to the commencement
of the fishing season, and made arrangements to
join a fishing party at the end of May to the
Schoodic lakes, which are situated in the State
of Maine.   On the 15th of May I was to start
for these lakes by steamer from St. John to St.
Stephen's; but being detained, I sent all my
traps and fishing gear with the rest of the party,
and I myself left St. John the same evening by
stage.

Of all the miserable means of locomotion, a
stage waggon in America is the most wretched.
The road was in parts very bad, and full of large

boulders. Luckily I was the only occupant of the vehicle, except the driver, and so had plenty of room. I was amused, on driving up to a place where we changed horses, at the remark of a loafer to the driver, on his paucity of passengers, "Why, you have quite a small crowd to-day, Jim."

Three people would be quite a crowd, and four or five a big crowd, in the Yankee parlance of the country; and this habit of calling everything by the most grandiloquent names strikes a stranger as being especially ridiculous. Every pothouse is an hotel, every village a city, and the most dirty eating-room a dining saloon.

I reached St. Stephen's at about nine o'clock the next morning, and went to an hotel to have some breakfast, where I joined the rest of our party. I found that I was rather late for the *table d'hote*—all meals at American hotels being on that plan—as, on being shown into the breakfast-room, I found all the servants of the establishment feeding on the remains. Fancy, in an English hotel, the servants being turned into the coffee-room, *en masse*, to feed! The servants at the hotels in this country are exceedingly touchy, and object to being called "waiter," or "boots," but expect to be addressed as "young man," or by their Christian name. I remember, on one occasion, when dining at an hotel in St. John, an officer, whom I shall name Captain Heavyswell, called to the waiter, during dinner, for a glass of beer. The man addressed "waiter," merely shouted to the bar-keeper, loud enough to be heard all over the room, " Pitcher of beer for Heavyswell."

After breakfast we all started by train for Louis Island, a small village situated on one of the lower Schoodic lakes, at a distance of about twenty miles. Here we hired Indians and canoes, and took the steamer to the head of the lake, about fifteen miles off. Having disembarked our luggage, we portaged to the upper lake, which is connected with the lower one by a stream three miles long. In this stream the trout congregate at certain times of the year, as also in the other streams connecting the chain of lakes, which extend some sixty miles up the country. We arrived at the head of the stream at sundown. Here was a lumber dam, and a large crew of men engaged in "driving" the timber brought down the lake in large rafts.

Whilst the Indians were putting up our tents, I made haste to put up my rod, and have a cast before dark—my first cast in American waters. In half an hour I had landed nine trout, averaging over two pounds each. These fish gave immense play, jumping high out of the water, several times on being hooked after the manner of sea trout at home. I may here say a word as to the species of trout in these lakes, as it has been a matter of a good deal of controversy between American naturalists, some of whom affirm that they are pent-up salmon. The St. Croix river, of which these lakes are the head waters, formerly abounded with salmon, but is now blocked up and quite impassible by the mill dams. I, for my part, do not for a moment suppose that these fish are salmon. In my opinion the idea is absurd, as there is nothing to prevent the fish going down to the sea; and when the river was blocked up in the first place, surely the fish then in the river would have followed their natural instinct, and returned to the salt water. Besides, I know plenty of rivers in North America from which the salmon have been shut out, and they contain no such fish. The trout in question are only like salmon in two respects, in colour and shape. I can only account for their being called salmon from the general ignorance of the people in America of natural history, and their common habit of calling birds and animals by their wrong appellations, merely because they have a slight resemblance to the animals they are named after. For instance, an American thrush (*turdus migratorius*) is called a robin, because it has a red breast; at the same time, it is the size and has the note of a thrush. I could enumerate many other like instances.

But to resume. On returning to camp much gratified with my trial of the fishing, I soon discovered that whilst I had been so occupied I had been most horribly bitten by musquitoes, which were in swarms everywhere. I had, in the innocence of my heart, worn a pair of knickerbockers; this was a lesson to me not to do so in future, as the musquitoes had stung me through my stockings in all directions.

There were some excellent casts near some

piles which were formed to guide the timber down the dam, and were filled up with stones above the water line. I found it a good plan to take up my station on one of these stands, with a good supply of rotten wood with which to make a fire with plenty of smoke, and so baffle the attacks of the musquitoes to a great extent. I remained at this place about a week, and had capital sport, killing with the fly one day sixty-three trout, of an average of two pounds each, few being smaller than one and a half pound, and none over three and a quarter pounds.

There were several camps of Yankees alongside of us, who were a great nuisance, following one about to any spot where they saw you successful, and fishing close to you with enormous flies, which fell with a great flop in the water. I managed to shake them off by fishing out of a canoe. These people were no sportsmen, and came out to have more what they call "a good time," and consume an unlimited quantity of liquor of the strongest kind.

To escape these annoyances, and for the sake of change, one of our party and myself made an excursion in canoes to the stream connecting the lake on which we were camped with the one above. After a paddle of about fifteen miles we arrived, towards evening, at our destination. The stream here, between the upper and lower lake, was only a few hundred yards in length, and very rapid and rocky, but with a capital pool both at the inlet and outlet.

The trout here rose so greedily that I continually hooked two at once; and the fish broke my casting line so often by jumping in different directions at the same moment, that I was obliged to fish with only one fly.

The scenery on our voyage up the lake was very pretty, the trees coming down to the water's edge. The foliage was very beautiful, and of a brighter green than one sees in England, the birch and white maple especially so.

I found that these trout took an artificial bait readily. I also caught with a spoon a togue (*salmo siskawitz*) of about six pounds. This fish is of the trout species, but never rises to a fly. They give no play, and their flesh is white, and very indifferent eating. They are sometimes caught as large as thirty pounds and upwards. I saw some specimens of the wood duck, so useful to the fly-makers, but was unable to bag one. Loons, also, were plentiful, with their peculiar weird-like note. I do not know anything more mournful, and at the same time more fascinating, than the cry of a loon on a still night, coming across a large lake, and echoing back among the forests.

The flies I found most killing in these waters were a light mallard wing, with red or orange body, and red cock's hackle. In the middle of the day, when the sun was bright, I did good execution with small greys and dark browns.

I was astonished at the ease and skill with which the Indians paddled their bark canoes, which were of the Milicite pattern—long, narrow, and crank. A single-bladed paddle is used; and one man at the stern, paddling from one side, both steers and propels the canoe with the same stroke. It looks very easy, but I, who was at that time quite a tyro as regards the woods, and had never been in a canoe before, on attempting to paddle one found myself describing small circles, nor did I feel exceedingly safe from turning a turtle at any moment.

However most things are to be learnt by

practice and perseverance ; since then many a mile have I paddled, many the hour have I stood up pole in hand forcing the frail birch bark up the foaming rapid where loss of balance would be an upset, and an upset the loss of one's tackle and perhaps the ruin of the expedition.

We kippered several hundred of the largest trout, which one of our Indians packed in a box made of spruce bark and sewn with the roots of the same tree.

The Indians were of the Milicite tribe, and a very lazy lot. One of our men, Joe by name, especially so. On one occasion after breakfast we paddled up the lake about four miles to try a brook for brown trout ; on our return in the evening, Joe appeared slower than usual, and on being asked why he did not paddle quicker, replied in very doleful accents, " Me had no breakfast, me had no dinner ; " the amount of pork and trout he had consumed at the first mentioned meal would have sufficed two ordinary men. Owing to a raft of timber which blocked up the end of the lake, we had to land and walk home about a mile. Joe being too idle to carry his canoe, left it on the beach.   Next morning he went to fetch it, and returning with a very long face, informed us in a whining voice, " Canoe spoilt.   Porcupine he eat him hole last night." Sure enough, the animal had evidently dined off the canoe, eating a large hole in the bark.

These Indians of the State of Maine were very exorbitant in their charges.   A dollar a day is the regular tariff, but the following year they wanted to charge a party from New Brunswick a dollar and a half per diem, expecting to receive it in gold or the equivalent, although no such stipulation was made.   The party at last agreed to give them what they demanded, but when pay day arrived, handed the Indians the amount in greenbacks, much to their disgust and discomfiture. As the premium was at that time very high they received in reality less than a dollar in gold. Some Yankees who were present at the time were much amused, and guessed the strangers " were pretty smart."

I consider the trout fishing in the Schoodic lakes the best in North America, for although there are plenty of both sea and brown trout to be killed in most of the streams, they do not

jump when hooked, and I have never met any
fish either at home or abroad, which for their
size gave equal play to these "lake shiners," as
they are called by the settlers. I learnt one
wrinkle by this trip—viz., how to dress for the
flies, which had punished me most severely. I
have never but in one place since found them so
numerous.

A person fresh from England always suffers at
first, the bites swelling very much, but after a
year or two one's blood seems to get accustomed
to the stings, for although they annoy at the
time, the swelling soon subsides and the irritation
is much less. There are many receipts for keeping off flies ; the most effective of any, and I
have tried most of them, is a mixture of hog's
lard and Stockholm tar, three parts of the former
and one of the latter mixed together. It easily
washes off, the grease preventing its sticking.
With a small box of this in my pocket I could
always in a few minutes render myself proof
against mosquitoes, black flies or sand flies, the
latter called by the Indians "bitum no seeum,"
are the worst of all, but are only very thick in
light soils. This specific requires to be renewed

about every hour.   A veil is also of great use
with a broad brimmed hat to keep it off one's
face ; but it is a great obstacle to the sight
which, when fly fishing, as I need not mention,
requires to be quick and sharp.

CHAPTER II.

Expedition to the Bay of Chaleurs—A Settler's fishing gear. No
sport in the Bay—Depart for Bathurst—Gaffing lobsters—Encamp
on the borders of the Nepisiguit—French settlers—The Rapids—
Fishing stations on the Nepisiguit—Bringing the Yankees to terms
—How to smoke salmon—Fishing in the Nepisiguit—Evenings on
the river.

On the 1st July of the same year I left St.
John on a salmon fishing expedition to the Bay
of Chaleurs accompanied by two brother officers,
Captains Butter and Coventry. We reached
Dalhousie by steamer from Shadiac.   Having
here hired three Miemac canoes and six Indians,
we chartered a schooner to drop us at the mouth
of the Cascapediac, a river some distance down
the Bay. We commenced the ascent of the
stream, each one in a canoe with two Indians to
pole, one at the stern, the other at the bow. The
stream was so rapid that although our men were
first-rate polers, we did not make more than ten

miles a day, and that without much delay except
for dinner at mid-day.   The way our canoes
were forced up the strongest rapids appeared to
us wonderful.   Of what use would a Rob Roy
be in such waters?   A Rob Roy canoe is a
cockney craft, fit only for the Thames or other
such sluggish waters, and easily to be paddled
by any muff.   In a country where the rivers
are the only roads, as in parts of America, it is
of no use whatever.

After a week's hard work we arrived at the
Forks, about sixty miles from the sea.   The river
for most of the way ran through a deep gorge,
with high and very steep mountains on each side,
wooded to the water's edge.   We caught plenty
of sea trout on our way up, some as heavy as
five pounds.   I met a settler coming down
the river with his canoe half full of them.   His
fishing gear was the most primitive I ever saw.
A stiff spruce pole served him for a rod, string
for a line, and his fly was a bunch of feathers
and red worsted fastened anyhow to a large
hook.   He had no reel, and on hooking a fish
hauled him at once by main force into his canoe.

We were much surprised and disappointed at

the paucity of salmon on our way up, and when
we reached the Forks only succeeded in killing
two, after several days fishing. We therefore
came to the conclusion that the river as regards
salmon was a myth, and decided to return to the
sea. It only took us one day to run down to
the salt water, so rapid was the stream, especially
at one place called " Indian falls," which we ran
in our canoes, and very ticklish work it was.

There are no settlers on the Cascapediac beyond a distance of ten miles from New Richmond,
the village at the river's mouth; here we hired
a schooner, and having embarked with our canoes
and Indians, set sail for Bathurst, a small village
situated at the mouth of the Nepisiguit river,
where we determined to try our luck ; getting
becalmed about twenty miles from Bathurst harbour we left the schooner, and prepared to paddle
along the coast, the rest of the distance. Going
ashore to have breakfast, we found swarms of lobsters in the shallow water among the rocks. We
succeeded in gaffing about thirty of them, these
made a welcome addition to our breakfast.

The number of lobsters all along the coasts
of North America is astonishing; there are

many companies who make a lucrative business by potting them.

After a long paddle we reached the head of the tide way of the Nepisiguit, late in the evening, where we made a fire and camped behind an old canoe lying on the shore; a canoe turned bottom up, makes a very good impromptu camp on a wet night.

The settlers here were for the most part French, some of them capital hands in canoes, and first-rate fishermen; although their tackle is bad, and their flies very indifferent, they kill many fish, as they know where the salmon lie to an inch, this in any stream is half the battle, as a rising fish will often take a seemingly worthless fly, especially if the man at the end of the rod knows how to place it over him.

The Nepisiguit is one of the most celebrated rivers in New Brunswick. The Indian name is " Winpigikewick," meaning troubled waters. The first three miles above the tide way is called "the rough waters;" this part of the stream is wide, and intersected by large rocks in all directions, forming most beautiful pools and "heights." The salmon here stand almost always on the ledges

of rock at the top of the rapids and "pitches," as a
small fall is called.   Some of these pitches are too
steep to pole up, but most of them can be run; to
do this requires nerve, and a steady hand, but is
not so difficult as it appears at first sight.   On
a subsequent visit to this river I was able to do
bow-man in a canoe, and poled up, and ran places
that appeared on my first visit extremely perilous
and difficult.   The canoes on this river are of
Micmac pattern, requiring two men, and are
quite steady enough to stand up in, and fish out
of.   Two miles above the rough waters are the
Round Rocks, which is a very fair fishing station
when the river is high and the fish are running.
Four miles above, at the bottom of the Pabneau
Falls, is a most excellent pool; the stream
at this spot is not more than twenty yards across,
and can be fished with a trout rod.   Here is that
famous cast from the flat rock, so well known to
all sportsmen who have visited the river.   We
camped within a few yards of this place, and
built a smoke house of spruce bark, as we decided
to make this our headquarters, one of us always
remaining here during our stay on the river.
Some Yankees were camped not far off, so we

sent to make arrangements to fish the flat-rock pool day about, as it was the best in the neigh-bourhood, these gentlemen refusing to come to any terms at all, we sent an ultimatum to the effect, that under these circumstances, one of us would sleep nightly on the flat rock to be ready for the morning cast. This threat was after-wards carried out, and was soon the means of bringing the Yankees to their bearings. We then made an amicable arrangement, and were good friends ever afterwards.

From the Pabineau to the Grand Falls is eleven miles. In this distance there are two good fishing stations—viz., Middle Landing and Chain of Rocks ; the former is an excellent pool in any water, and easily to be fished ; the latter is good only in high water. Grand Falls is the best station on the river, containing four good pools ; it was, on our arrival, occupied by a party, so we were unable to fish there until a short time before our departure from the river. The salmon cannot get above the Grand Falls, though steps might be made, and there is sixty miles length of river above, and excellent spawning grounds. There are, however, great quantities

of brown trout above, especially at a place
called the "Devil's Elbow," where they are large,
some weighing three and four pounds. During
our stay on the river, which lasted a month, we
smoked over a hundred and twenty salmon, which
we packed in boxes and sent off to our friends
at St. John. The following is the receipt for
that process :—Split the fish down the back and
clean them, cutting out the gills at the same
time ; this should be done as soon as possible
after they are caught, or the fish will become
soft ; immerse for two days in a strong pickle of
salt and water, a trough for this purpose is easily
hewn out of a fallen spruce or pine, or, in lieu,
use a dish of birch or spruce bark. After taking
the fish out of the pickle, wash them in running
water, then hang them up in a smoke house for
six days. A smoke house is built in the shape
of a wigwam, and covered with birch or spruce
bark ; great care must be taken to keep the fire,
which is placed in the smoke house, always
burning very slowly, if it gets too hot the fish
become cooked and therefore spoilt ; it is a good
plan to place the entrails of fish on the fire to
keep it cool.

The scenery on the Nepisiguit, though pretty, has very little grandeur about it, the land being comparatively flat on both sides of the river, which with the breadth and shallowness of the stream in many parts, soon causes the water to become hot after a drought, when the fish naturally become sulky, and will not rise. I remember once, under these circumstances, whipping the stream for four days without a rise, although there were many salmon up at the time. I consider this river therefore most uncertain, though if one is lucky enough to hit off the right height of water, excellent sport is to be had.

The flies for the Nepisiguit are of a plain description, especially as regards the wings, which should be brown mallard, with a few sprigs of golden pheasant neck feather underneath ; body fiery brown with blue and claret hackle, wound on together, is a standard fly, and is known by the name of the " Nicholson," so called after the inventor, a well-known sportsman of St. John, New Brunswick. Black body, black hackle and yellow tip is a killer, and the same fly with a crimson tip fishes well at Middle Landing. Grey monkey body and Irish grey hackle is very good in clear water. Body half grey, half claret fur, with grey and claret hackles placed on together, is an admirable fly for the Pabineau. This fly was invented by my friend Captain Coventry, who stuck many a fish with it off the Flat Rock.

The climate is charming in the summer, hot days succeeded by most lovely still evenings, which you can never so thoroughly enjoy as when camped alongside a noble river, smoking your after supper pipe ; you listen to the shrill cry of the mosquito hawks (a species of night jar); and the notes of the frogs, which vary from a shrill whistle to the hoarse croak of the bull frog, intermingled with the pleasant sound of running water. Your rod, ready for the morning cast, is leaning against a bush ; at length you lie down to rest, speculating where you will rise him in the morning, and determined not to miss that fish which comes up by the white stone, as you did yesterday.

CHAPTER III.

Second Expedition to the Bay of Chaleurs—The inquisitive Storekeeper
—a type of the settling class—Leave for the Restigouche and
Metapedia — Quality of the sport —Milisite Canoes—Want of
protection of the rivers—Necessity of enforcing the Fishery Laws
—Instances of the carelessness of the officials—How to protect
the rivers—Advantages of the American waters for sport.

THE following year I paid another visit to the
Bay of Chaleurs, and on the 6th of August
reached the mouth of the river Bonaventure,
having paddled along the coast in a Micmac
canoe with two Indians from Dalhousie, a distance
of fifty miles. We had employed one of my
Indians, named Peter Grey, during the previous
year ; he was a good poler and knew how to
gaff salmon, which is an art that few Indians
understand; their idea being to strike him dead
in the water, not to land him, consequently many
is the fish they have lost me.

The settlers along the south shore of the Bay

of Chaleurs are almost exclusively French. They both farm and fish—chiefly the latter. Their implements of husbandry are most primitive; they are far behind either the British or the German population, and appear never to improve.

At Bonaventure I was much amused by the inquisitiveness of a storekeeper, who, when asked to change a sovereign, was evidently puzzled as to who or what I was. I was got up in a smock and trowsers of blue drill, which I found to be the best dress for the mosquitos, as being both light and impervious to their stings; the ends of my trowsers were tucked into my socks to prevent any ingress at that point, of black flies or other villainous winged insects; my head gear was a broad brimmed Yankee felt hat. The man first asked me if I wanted anything out of the store? Answer—No. Did I belong to any of the schooners in the harbour? No. Where did I come from? Dalhousie. Did I belong there? No. Was I a native of the country? No. What brought me out there? Because I was sent. What was I doing? Salmon fishing. "Why that won't pay?" "It pays me." Had I anyone with me? Yes, two Indians. Did these men assist me in any way? I was not likely to keep them if they did not. Was I sure I wanted nothing out of the store? Not to-day, but I should be obliged if he would change me twenty sovereigns to-morrow. I then left him, more mystified than ever.

These people can never understand one's going to any trouble or expense for mere sport—the almighty dollar is always uppermost in their minds.

Next morning on presenting myself at the store, my friend of the previous evening was exceedingly civil and offered me a drink, having in the meantime discovered from the Indians who I was. But he looked rather foolish when I entered his shop.

The great peculiarity of the Bonaventure is the exceeding clearness of the water, which is signified by its Indian name. At the depth of twenty feet I could distinguish between the head and tail of a new coin. After fishing a few days with but indifferent success, and finding that the run of fish had passed, I paddled eighteen miles to Pasbeiac, a fishing station further along the coast, and arrived there just in time to catch the

Canadian steamer which dropped me at Dalhousie.
On leaving the steamer I immediately paddled
up the Restigouche as far as Campbelton, a
village eighteen miles from the mouth. We
arrived here at two o'clock a.m., and making a
fire on the beach, were soon fast asleep. The
next day we continued our course up stream,
which was not very rapid until we got to where
the Metapedia joins the main river ; after paddling about five miles up the Metapedia, a very
rapid stream, I camped near two good salmon
pools. I remained a fortnight at this spot and
had some fair sport, though here, as with the
Bonaventure, I was rather late for the best run,
which takes place in July.

The flies for the Restigouche and its tributaries are rather more gaudy than those
used in the Nepisiguit ; orange body with claret
hackle ; body half black, half orange, with black
hackle and yellow shoulder ; body half black,
half crimson, with black hackle and jay shoulder;
with all of these mixtures use a rather gaudy
mixed wing, with sprigs of wood duck, and red
macaw feelers.

There is good fishing in the Quatawamkedg-

wick, another tributary of the Restigouche, falling
into that river forty miles above the Metapedia.

The worst of the Restigouche is, that the pools
are very few, and about thirty miles apart, but
the fish are larger than those of any river in
the province.

The Mirimichi, which flows into the Bay of
Chaleurs, at the town of Chatham, one of the
chief ship building localities in the Provinces, is
a fine stream, having many large tributaries
heading far back in the heart of the country.
I made a trip up this river on one occasion, and
had some very good sport. Burnt Hill, about
forty miles from Boistown, is the best station,
where are some excellent pools ; ten miles above
is Slate Island, also a good place, and higher
up still are " Louis Falls; " there are also many
other pools where fish are met with.

The Mirimichi is a very difficult river to pole,
owing to the great number of rocks and rapids.
At the time I went up the river we brought
Milicite canoes and Indians from Fredericton,
there being neither on the river. The settlers
use "dug-outs" (canoes hewn from single trees),
but I prefer a birch canoe and Indians whom

I have been in the habit of employing. I remember polling bow all the way up, and very hard work it was, particularly getting up what are called the "Three Mile Rapids," which are one continued length of rocks and broken water for that distance. Near the top is the worst place of all, called by the settlers "Shove and be d——d."

A Milicite canoe is much more crank than a Micmac, and is difficult to stand up in at any time, unless to one accustomed to it. The flies for this river are plain; grey body, with mallard or turkey wings, is one of the standard patterns. Most Nepisiguit flies are also adapted for this water. The salmon are about the same size as those in that river, namely, from ten to fifteen pounds, and some few are larger. The country bordering the Mirimichi is more hilly than the Nepisiguit, and the banks of the river are steep in many places.

Along the coast, half way between the mouths of this river and the Nepisiguit, is the Tabusintack, a small river with few or no salmon, but celebrated for its sea trout, beyond all other streams in the province. One hundred or more trout may be killed in a day by a single rod, and they weigh from one to four pounds. But one soon gets tired of such sport.

All the rivers in New Brunswick are very much damaged by over netting, both in the tide way, along the coast, and also in the fresh water. At first it appears a miracle how any salmon can manage to pass the labyrinth of nets, set with hardly any restriction ; for although there are very fair fishery laws, they are but seldom enforced. The fish wardens are for the most part useless, their appointments sinecures, and mere political jobs. The following is an instance of the way some of these gentlemen do, or rather do not, do their duty :—I met an Indian when on the Restigouche, who had been hired by the warden of the river, to take him up in a canoe on his one annual inspection, which I suppose he required to enable him to satisfy his conscience, on pocketing his salary, some £40 per annum. The individual in question called at the houses of the different owners of nets, and after informing them of their proper legal length, without inspecting the same, finished up by asking for a salmon. Having made about twenty such like visits, not forgeting the salmon, he returned home and drew his salary. Some of the wardens are proprietors of nets, and do not trouble their heads how they are set, provided they catch fish.

Several years ago when I was in New Bruns. wick, the proprietor of a net at Bathurst was prosecuted by the warden for having the mesh of an illegal size. The delinquent wrote to a friend of his, then a member of the Legislative Assembly of New Brunswick, and representative of his county. This honorable member managed to get the law altered, so as to make the net of a legal mesh, not only this, but he made the law retrospective, in the mean time staying further proceedings. Such a state of things speaks for itself.

The only way to protect the fisheries is to abolish the wardens as now appointed, who are chiefly farmers, and have other things to attend to.

Appoint one head inspector for each province, and let him have under his control a staff of water bailiffs, strong active fellows, able to pole either a birch or log canoe, and with suffi-cient pay to enable them to relinquish all other employment and traverse the rivers and coasts by day and night during the fishing season. By this means poachers would easily be dropped on, and a fear established. For although the settlers talk very big of what they would do in the event of their being interfered with in their illegal practices, yet no people have a more wholesome dread of the law when they know it will be enforced.

Great things are now expected from the " New Dominion," and I hope that the protection of the rivers, and the proper carrying out of the fishery laws will be amongst them.

One great drawback is, that with a few exceptions the inhabitants are not sportsmen, and would rather make one dollar than enjoy the sport of killing a hundred salmon.

However, I think things are about to mend in New Brunswick, as the present Governor of that province is fully alive to the importance of protecting the salmon, not only as a source of amusement, but of food and wealth to the country.

A great advantage in the North American rivers is, that they cannot, as at home, be poached by spearing and gaffing in the winter ; at that season, Jack Frost proves an effectual keeper.

CHAPTER IV.

FINDING the fishing on the Metapedia getting slack I resolved to carry out my original intention of calling moose, the time for which, the 1st of September, was drawing near. This sport of which I had heard such exciting tales, more than justified by after experience, I was most anxious to try.

Leaving my camp on the Metapedia, I ran down the river to Campbelton. On the opposite shore is the chief Indian village, and Government allotment to the Micmac Indians who inhabit the northern part of the province. The Milicite tribe occupies the south, especially the St. John waters, their head quarters being on that river, fifteen miles above Fredericton.

The Indian village at Campbelton is no mere accumulation of bark wigwams, but includes a considerable number of very fair cottages, with land attached to many of them. Some of these Indians farm, and keep cows, and most of them are well off and decently clothed. The village also boasts of a chapel and school, in charge of a priest, who is paid by the Government. I may mention that all the Indians in the provinces are Roman Catholics, having been formerly converted by the French Jesuits ; but whether they are, at the present time, in favour of the new dogma of the infallibility of the Pope, I cannot say ; being ignorant and superstitious, they probably believe everything they are told.

This description of the Red man, will, no doubt, appear charming to some persons, but I must confess that for my part, I prefer the man living in a bark wigwam, wearing a pair of mocassins in place of boots, the rest of his attire more or less patched, without regard to uniformity of either texture or colour.

A half finished canoe outside his door looks business-like, which, together with an old deer skin and a steel trap or two, leads one to suppose the man is of some use in the woods ; but strange as it may appear, not more than one Indian in twenty, in these days, is able to build a canoe.

On the other hand, the man with the cows and farm knows nothing, having lost the craft of the hunter, and imperfectly learnt that of the farmer ; he probably knows how to make a butter tub, but has never learnt the art of canoe making ; he understands little or nothing of trapping, and might as well try to call an elephant as a moose. Unfortunately the genus hunter is dying out ; the young Indians are too idle to go into the woods, and the old men cannot last for ever.

It was not without a considerable amount of trouble that I at last succeeded in finding an old Indian of the name of Noel, who was able to call moose. I had some discussion with this man as to the best hunting ground and the means of reaching it. It was at length decided to proceed to the lakes at the head of the river Nepisiguit.

Noel assisted me in making this decision by maps of the country drawn by him on sheets of birch bark with a burnt stick.

Before giving an account of hunting the moose, a short description of that animal will, perhaps, not be out of place :—The moose, or North American elk, (*cervus alces*) is identical with the European animal of that species, with the exception that the American elk is of rather a darker color. This point, which has been a matter of controversy among naturalists, has been indisputably settled by Captain Campbell Hardy, R.A. The moose, almost black in summer, is in the winter months of a lighter shade ; his hair is long and coarse, particularly on the mane, which sticks up like bristles when the animal is enraged, or otherwise excited ; under the throat there is a tuft of hair ; in the male this tuft or bell, as it is called, is more than a foot in length. A full grown bull moose often weighs fifteen hundred pounds ; he stands six· teen or seventeen hands high ; his legs are slight for so large a body, but of immense strength, and his capabilities of jumping are surprising. He rarely breaks into a galop, but at a swinging trot will clear a height of many feet. One of the chief characteristics of this animal is the mouffle, or over hanging lip, which gives to his head an ugly appearance; his hoofs are sharp and pointed, his horns palmated, and they sometimes measure six feet across; their surface is rough, and they have been known to weigh seventy pounds. The moose casts his antlers, which commence to grow in April, yearly; the old bulls drop them as early as November, the younger animals later.

The meat is excellent, having a flavour of gamey beef; the mouffle is considered a great delicacy. The skin, which makes tough leather, is in great request for mocassins. The food of the moose, consists chiefly of the shoots and bark of young hard wood trees; the height of these animals enables them to reach some distance, and their weight to bend down small trees by sliding over them with their bodies, and so to strip off the bark and twigs. In summer time they hang about the neighbourhood of muddy lakes and sluggish brooks—called "dead waters," to which they repair, plunging into the water up to their necks, for the purpose of escaping the flies, and feeding on the roots of water lilies, or other aquatic plants. At this time of year the bulls are solitary, the cows accompanied by their calves.

At the approach of the rutting season, which begins in September, the males leave off feeding, and rub the velvet from their horns by scraping them against the trees ; they also dig holes in the ground with their fore-feet, rolling themselves in the earth they have scattered about. I have seen places in the woods where the brutes have been disporting themselves in this manner, treading down the bushes, scraping up the earth, and rubbing against the trees with their horns.

During the rutting season, which lasts until the middle of October, the males follow about the females. On the fall of the first snow in November, the moose begin to " yard," as it is called, namely, to take up their station on the side of some hard wood hill, where the moose-wood, birch, maple and other trees on which they delight to feed, are plentiful. In the absence of hard wood growth, they will yard in any place where food is to be had. A yard consists of generally three or four animals ; cows

and young bulls yard together, the old bulls,
alone. If these animals are not disturbed they
will remain the whole winter feeding about in
one place, never perhaps moving more than a
mile from where they originally took up their
quarters ; so that a hunter finding a yard may
always put off hunting the animals until a
favourable day, without fear of their decamping,
unless frightened by man. If once disturbed
they will travel miles before yarding afresh. On
the approach of spring, when the snow and ice
melt, the cows go off by themselves to calve.

The horns of the moose are at their prime
when he has reached the age of about nine or
ten years, after that time they get stumpy and
deteriorate.

Having left my "half-tent" and all other
superfluous baggage behind, I started from Campbelton at the end of August, taking two canoes.
My Indians were Noel, Peter and another man.
Two of us in each canoe poled twenty miles up
the Restigouche. We then turned up the Upsalquitch, a tributary of that river, and falling into
it on its right bank.

The Upsalquitch is a moderate sized river,

containing few salmon and those of small size. In this stream we speared some white-fish, a species peculiar to North America, and excellent eating; they do not rise to a fly and seldom exceed two pounds in weight.

We continued our course up the river, which was quite unsettled, camping at night on the banks. This, in fine weather, merely consisted of making a fire in some sheltered spot and laying down a bed of fir boughs. After eating supper, and smoking a pipe, I rolled myself in a blanket, and slept soundly till day break.

There is a charm in this manner of travelling in a wild country, known only to those who have experienced it. Something fresh appears in view at every turn of the stream; all talking or other noise must be avoided, as at any moment an animal may make its appearance, perhaps a moose coming down to drink, or a bear to feed on the berries that grow on the dog wood, and other plants found in the vicinity of water. In the course of six days, having journeyed seventy miles from the mouth of the river, which was easy poling most of the way, though my hands got very much blistered, we reached the " por-

tage," (viz., a place where you leave a river or
lake to travel by land to another), at this spot
we left our canoes, and prepared to carry our
luggage through thick woods without a road of
any kind to lake Nictor, one of the heads of the
Tobique, distant twenty-five miles.

The Indian fashion of carrying your hunting
paraphernalia, also the way in which they make
up a bundle is peculiar, at the same time it is by
far the best and easiest method of transporting a
load ; a cockney tourist, with the latest thing in
knapsacks, would not carry a third of the weight.

The following is the Indian plan :—A blanket
is spread on the ground, across which is laid a
strap two feet broad in the middle, with long
narrow thongs attached. The thongs are placed
about two feet apart, the sides of the blanket are
then turned inwards over the thongs ; the different
articles to be carried being placed in a compact
heap in the centre, the two ends of the strap are
then drawn tight on either side and fastened
together. The blanket is thus drawn up at the
edges, in the middle it is lapped over and fastened
by wooden pegs; the broad part of the strap should
be sufficiently loose to enable it to go over both

shoulders and across the chest when carrying this bundle ; an axe stuck in the belt and a rifle on the shoulder complete the load.

Having collected all our luggage into four bundles made up as above described, we set out on our journey. Our loads were heavy, and weighed over eighty pounds each, although I had diminished my kit to the lowest ebb. For one must eat, and flour and pork are heavy articles, not to mention ammunition, blankets, kettles and other things.

Travelling through woods with a load is tedious and often most aggravating. The continued scrambling over fallen trees, which are sometimes rotten and give way with the weight, the constant pushing through a thick undergrowth of alder or moose-wood together with frequent falls, form a combination of evils most trying to the temper. You are not looking out when a bough, bent down by the man directly in front, springs back and cuts you a wipe on the face. Again you come to a brook with a tree fallen across, looking as if placed there purposely to form a bridge, when half way over you loose your balance and come down on your back in the water. This accident happened to myself the day after we left the banks of the river ; I was as helpless as a sheep on its back, and had to be hauled out by the Indians, who laughed a good deal at my absurd position.

I was a novice at "lugging,"—the local term used to denote carrying on the back—so found it hard at first, but after a time became quite accustomed to it. It is the usual plan when lugging in the woods, to set out after an early breakfast ; in the middle of the day a halt is made for dinner, then on again until near dusk, when it is time to think of camping for the night.

On the evening of the fourth day since we had left the Upsalquitch, I was delighted to see the long wished-for waters of lake Nictor gleaming through the trees. The journey proved longer than I had anticipated from Noel's map of the country. Distance in the woods always appears greater than it really is, there being nothing whatever to mark your progress. Several times I questioned Noel as to how far we were from the lake, all the answer he gave was "a good piece yet ;" this means anything from two miles to ten.

The woods we had passed through in our route

from the Upsalquitch were principally of mixed growth, with some hard wood ridges ; "hard wood" in America meaning all trees that do not belong to the fir tribe, they on the other hand being designated "soft wood." Hard wood growth, consisting principally of larch, birch, maple, with a few pines and firs intermingled, is generally found on the uplands, where is the best soil. The low lands are mostly covered with a mixture of hard and soft wood. In some parts the latter entirely predominates.

In winter time the soft wood growth is commonly known as the "green woods." It is a curious fact that where hard wood growth has been destroyed by fire, or cleared by the axe, soft wood springs up spontaneously and *vice versa.* In parts of the Baltic coast, now covered with the fir tribe, numbers of oak trees are discovered embedded in the soil.

We camped near lake Nictor, and during the night I had a narrow and providential escape from a falling tree, which, when we were all asleep, fell right across our camp ; fortunately it caught on a log by the fire, so I escaped with a slight bruise, otherwise Peter and myself would have been crushed to death.   As it was we were pinned to the earth, another inch or two would have broken his neck and my legs.   I got up in the night before this accident happened, and was on the point of putting the log that saved us on the fire, but luckily changed my mind !

The scenery at lake Nictor is very beautiful, consisting of the usual forests of maple, birch and fir reaching down to the water's edge ; this part of the country had not at that time been visited by the axe of the "lumberer" — woodcutter. The stately pines still towered here and there far above the other trees.   To the north a high mountain with top devoid of trees rose up majestically, adding to the wildness and beauty of the scene.

Finding an old bark canoe left by some hunters, we patched it up and proceeding to the head of the lake portaged the canoe together with our other luggage three miles, when we came upon the uppermost lake of the chain, forming the main source of the river Nepisiguit.   This chain is composed of three lakes two or three miles in length and connected by short streams.   A more admirably adapted spot for moose calling could

not be found, but to my disappointment the chief
requisite was wanting, — the presence of the
animals themselves, nor could we discover any
fresh moose " sign " in the neighbourhood. We
tried calling on several very suitable nights
without any response.

The woods near these lakes a few years back
were celebrated for moose, but a number of Indians
the previous winter had made much havoc among
them by the abominably unsportsmanlike practice
of running them down in the deep snow where
they cannot escape.   Moreover these hunters took
only the hides leaving the carcases to rot, the
smell of which in the spring has the effect of
driving away any moose that are left in the
vicinity.   There was ample evidence of the
slaughter that had taken place in the piles of
moose hair lying near old camps, of which I came
across several on the margin of the lakes.   I
caught in these lakes plenty of trout—small,
though of good quality.

Noel now informed me that we should find
moose at the head of the Sevogle river, I therefore
determined to go there, or anywhere so long as
moose could be found.

Leaving the lakes we ran down the Nepisiguit
in our canoe, and a dug-out we had picked up.
After descending the stream about twenty-five
miles we halted where the south-east branch of
the Nipisiguit joins the main river.

We passed several beaver dams on our way
down, but did not stop to meddle with them ; I
shot a couple of black ducks, and near the junction
of the two streams caught with a fly some fine
brown trout, several of which were over three
pounds in weight.

Our provisions were now getting low ; fortunately I was able to replenish our stock from a
"lumber" camp in the neighbourhood, where we
found flour, pork, and molasses stored up for the
next winter, when a crew of men would occupy
the camp for the purpose of cutting timber.

Leaving our canoe and dug-out on the bank
of the river we made a fresh start for the new
hunting ground, lugging as before heavy loads.
Just before setting out we were joined by a party
of nine Indians on their way up to hunt beaver
on the Sevogle waters and murder moose on the
snow becoming deep, late in the winter.

In parts of the country we passed through the

woods were very thick, especially at one place.
Here we had to cross three miles of burnt land,
and the trees lay piled in all directions on the
top of each other.   It was impossible to go three
yards without having to climb over a fallen spruce
or fir with the dead branches sticking up, catching
in our clothes and poking us in the face.   The
day was hot, and falling several times I felt as a
Yankee would say, " quite mad."   At last after
several hours of toil we extricated ourselves from
this " Slough of Despond," and throwing off our
bundles took a rest, with its invariable accompani-
ment, a pipe.

At the end of six days' journey from the time
of leaving the Nepisiguit, we came to a small lake
where the nine Indians left us.   Here we were
glad to see fresh moose " sign," and called at night
alongside a beaver dam, situated in a brook flowing
out of the lake.   At this spot I had for the first
time an opportunity of seeing a beaver.   These
curious animals swim about their ponds in the
evening, several did so on this occasion ; one in
particular sat on a log forty yards off eating some
roots, which from time to time he fished up from
the bottom of the pond.   I refrained from firing,

4

as the noise would have disturbed any moose in
the neighbourhood.

Noel had called several hours without an answer,
so at length I fired at a beaver swimming in the
water (it was moon-light), but missed him, the
ball passing over his head. " No good wait any
longer," observed Noel, " beavers no come out
any more ; he tell him other beavers in house."
We waited a short time and his words proved true,
for no more beavers made their appearance. I
have no doubt the one fired at communicated his
fears to his companions.

The next morning we broke the dam, killing
two beavers, of which I shot one as it was
escaping over the top of the dam, where I was
stationed in readiness by Noel. The same evening we set steel traps both at the inlet and
outlet of the pond, and next morning had a
beaver in each trap ; one animal had nearly
escaped by knawing off the foot by which he was
caught. These beavers were a great addition
to our larder ; the tail is one of the greatest
delicacies to be met with in any country, and
makes soup as good as turtle. The flesh is fair,
but requires to be boiled twice in water, freshly

replenished, or it tastes strong ; but we were glad to get fresh meat of any description, having, with the exception of a grouse and four ducks, lived on salt pork for the last three weeks.

The next evening we camped at the foot of a high mountain on which there was not a tree ; on walking up to the top I had a magnificent view of the surrounding country. It was one glorious panorama of forests interspersed with lakes and rivers as far as the eye could reach. The high ridges were principally hard wood ; in the low lands the fir tribe was most numerous. The surface of the mountain was rocky, covered with large granite boulders; cranberries, of which I collected a quantity, were also plentiful.

Our stock of provisions again becoming small, I sent off Peter for flour, &c., to a lumber camp distant about thirty miles.

CHAPTER V.

Arrival at the Sevogle waters—Description of scenery—Moose tracks
—Pleasures of moose calling—Delight at bagging my first moose
—Encamp in the woods—Our provisions run short—Indians arrive to our assistance—Decrease of moose, and cause of it—Incidents on the journey back to St. John—The sport of moose calling defended—The three classes who attack it, and their argu-
ments answered—Advice to those going moose calling—How a
Governor of Novia Scotia missed sport—Vaiious methods of hunting the moose—Remarks on the practice of " Running down."

THE following day we reached the lake at the
head of the Sevogle river, for which we were
bound. At this place I was delighted to see
plenty of moose sign, their paths round the lake
being trodden down and much used. The evening was favourable for calling ; so, accompanied
by Noel I proceeded to the inlet of the lake,
which was bordered on one side, by " barrens,"
(often called plains) several miles in length ; on
the other by woods. These barrens are open
spots in the woods, varying in extent from an

acre to several square miles. They are fringed by a growth of dwarf tamarac, (American larch) and spruce ; the latter, in many places is dotted over the surface of the barren, which is generally more or less marshy.

Finding a large fallen tree close to the water's edge, on the side of the lake bordered by the barrens, Noel pitched upon it as a good station for our operations. Except in a canoe, a better spot for calling could not be discovered. The country bordering the lake was flat, surrounded at about two miles distant by high hills. The night was beautifully clear, the air frosty, and intense stillness prevailed, broken only by the hooting of an owl, the loud splash of a beaver striking the water with his tail, or the plunge of a musk rat in the lake.

The wailing note of the female moose admirably imitated by Noel, with his horn of winter birch bark, rolled over the lake and barrens, and echoed back from the surrounding hills. Between each call, which was repeated about every fifteen minutes, we listened with drawn breath ; for upwards of an hour there was no response. Suddenly the Indian pointing with his "caller"

towards the end of the barrens, ejaculated in a
low voice "Hear him ; " I listened intently, and
from afar, fully three miles away, was just able
to distinguish the short guttural call of a bull
moose.   Oh, welcome sound ! far more sweet
than that of any musical instrument invented
since the days that David played before Saul.
Noel called again at intervals, the moose answering, his response becoming gradually more dis-
tinct as he approached.

I now placed myself about fifty yards a-head
of the Indian, taking advantage of a stunted
spruce as cover.   Half an hour elapsed, the answers becoming nearer and nearer.   Now and
then the moose dashed his horns against the
trees, producing a loud crash.   At length I
caught sight of his dusky form coming straight
towards me, but when within about one hundred
yards he stopped.   At this juncture, the Indian,
who was on the margin of the lake, imitated
with his axe the noise made by an animal walking in the water.   On hearing this, the bull,
whose hesitation seemed at once to vanish, gave
a loud call, and advanced several yards nearer.
There he stood, pawing the earth and snorting.

His antlers in the uncertain light, resembled
the roots of a torn up tree. My nerves were
strung to the highest pitch of excitement; now
the long wished for moment had arrived; slowly
raising my gun, I fired. The animal gave a
tremendous plunge and suddenly turning round,
made for the woods. The contents of my other
barrel followed him in his flight.

I was almost sure that he was hit; but hor-
rible thought! if I should have missed him, and
lost such a pair of horns? However, there was
nothing to be done until morning, so, having
smoked a pipe, I lay down in my blanket. An
hour before day-light Noel commenced to call
again, but the wind getting up, made it useless.

There is not much chance of getting an answer
after eleven o'clock at night, as the animals lie
down about that hour, until shortly before day-
break. From that hour till morning or even
after it is light, is the best time to call; and
should the moose make his appearance when it is
light, or even partially so, there is, of course, a
much better chance of killing him.

We rose with the dawn, and tracked the moose
to the edge of the woods, which were two hun-

dred yards distant. On reaching the spot where the animal had entered the forest, Noel made an exclamation and holding up a leaf with blood on it, said, " Moose him hit." A little further on we discovered where he had lain down, there, also, were marks of blood. " He feel pretty bad," said Noel, " he not go far." After following his tracks for a couple of hundred yards further, we came to a thicket of young firs. Aha ! what is that dark mass on the ground just distinguishable through the trees ? There he lay dead, a fine bull, with splendid horns. One ball had passed through his lungs, the other inflicting a flesh wound in the neck. Thus, at last, after numerous disappointments, the toil of many days through the pathless forests, was rewarded. Having cut out a steak for breakfast, we returned to the place where we had deposited our bundles on the previous day.

I determined to take up my quarters in this locality ; so we built a double bark camp in the woods, a mile from the lake. It took us a couple of days to finish this habitation, and transport thither the best part of the moose, together with the skin, head, &c. The skin was stretched on poles, and the meat, after being cut into thin strips, was hung up to smoke on a stage made for the purpose.

On a subsequent evening we called up another moose within forty yards, though, unfortunately, I was unable to see him, on account of some alder bushes that intervened. I heard the rustling of his horns among the bushes, and expected him to emerge every moment ; but after waiting for fully ten minutes, a crack of a stick was heard about a quarter of a mile off. " He gone," said Noel, " smell us."

The next morning I saw by his tracks where the moose had stopped, and then turned back. How that great beast with his horns, could sneak off, without making the slightest noise, is a marvel. But I have since found, they always manage to do so, when frightened on coming up to a call.

Young bulls often never answer at all, but come sneaking up, as still as mice. They approach in this stealthy and silent manner through fear of the larger bulls, who, should they come in contact with them, would soon send them to the right about,

It was now getting towards the end of September, and after several sharp frosts, the woods were clothed in all the magnificence of their autumnal beauty. The verdure of the forest was changed into brilliant scarlet, rich violet, every shade of blue and brown, vivid crimson, and glittering yellow. Trees of the fir tribe, alone, retained their unchangeable dark green.

We had, by this time, consumed almost all our provisions ; and the Indian who had gone for flour, &c., had not returned. In addition, we had a week of very wet and boisterous weather, which prevented all chance of sport, and the moose meat would not dry on account of the rain, and so became tainted.

In a couple more days we had eaten the last of our flour, pork, tea, sugar, and salt, and worst of all, our tobacco had come to an end. We had nothing now to live on but the tainted meat ; if we had had any salt and tobacco remaining, I should not have cared. Already I had turned out the pockets of my old shooting jacket, and smoked the tobacco dust there accumulated. Gun-powder became a substitute for salt, and dry leaves for tobacco. The beavers declined to enter our traps, and we were unable to find any grouse.

At length, after four days of this starvation diet, going to bed hungry, without any prospect of breakfast on the morrow, Peter arrived with provisions, and glad, indeed, we all were to eat a good meal.

The reason of Peter's long absence was, that he had lost his way for some time, and on reaching the lumber camp at last, had found it unoccupied ; he was, therefore, obliged to go down to the settlements, fifty miles distant, before he could get any supply of food. At one time he had nothing but a grouse to last him three days. I did not pity him much, as Indians ought not to lose their way in the woods, except in a snow storm, and then only for a short time.

We remained, altogether, a fortnight in this place, trapping beaver, and, whenever the night was still, calling moose. I got two more shots, killing one moose and missing another in the dark. As the latter was only a young bull, and had but small horns, I did not take it to heart. The call of a young bull can be distinguished from that of an older animal, being less gutteral and in a higher key, at a distance it somewhat resembles the noise of chopping with an axe. One night we heard two moose fighting, and a tremendous crashing they made. With the beaver we were pretty successful, nine of which we trapped.

There are some magnificent pines in the neighbourhood of the lake, the largest I have ever seen. This part of the country has never been "lumbered," being too difficult of access and devoid of streams of sufficient size to float down the lumber.

There was a great scarcity of ducks in this part of the country and of cariboo—we had met but one track during all our wanderings. The moose seemed entirely to monopolize the woods, though they and cariboo do not interfere with each other, like hares and rabbits in England.

At the time I am now writing I should probably not find one single moose in these "regions," so great has been the destruction of those animals in the early spring, by Indians running them down for their mere hides.

My leave now drawing to a close, we left the lake and portaged our horns, skins, &c., nearly twenty miles to a lumber camp, which we were fortunate enough to find occupied by a party of lumberers. These men, who had only arrived the previous day, received us with great hospitality. All my Indians, with the exception of Peter, now returned to the woods for the purpose of trapping during the coming winter.

Leaving most of my kit at the camp in charge of the head man, who promised to forward them to me, I set off with Peter for Newcastle. We carried only our guns and horns, but they weighed quite enough. After a walk of thirty miles in torrents of rain, and after crossing with great difficulty several swollen rivers, we arrived late at night at an Indian camp a few miles from Newcastle. We put up at the home of Julien, the head man of the village, who was most accommodating and procured us a good supper.

The next day this man took us down to Newcastle in his canoe. On arriving at that town I went to an hotel and ordered some refreshment, tendering my last dollar note as payment. The note was so torn and dirty that the landlord declined to take it, and suggested my getting it changed at the bank across the

street. This was rather awkward, for I did not
know any one at Newcastle, and my dress was
certainly no recommendation : home-spun trowsers, one knee patched with a shot bag, the other
with a piece of blue drill picked up in a lumber
camp ; socks made from the remains of several
pairs sewn together ; mocassins, ditto ; a home-
spun smock faded and dirty ; these, together
with an extremely dilapidated and battered old
wide-awake, completed my attire. However,
proceeding to the bank I introduced myself to
the manager who was exceedingly civil, cashed
me a cheque at once, and asked me to come over
in the evening and have a pipe and a glass of
grog.

On returning to the hotel I found the landlord
had during my absence pumped Peter. I was
accordingly received with the greatest civility,
put up in the best room of the house, and had a
private sitting room placed at my disposal. The
landlord informed me with pride that his father
had been an old soldier, and had served through
the whole of the Peninsular war. In the evening
I strolled up to the house of the manager of the
bank. The bell was answered by a lady who

eyed me rather suspiciously, and replied in answer to my inquiries that Mr. ——— was out, and that I had better call the next day. I had not the cheek to introduce myself, so departed. On the way back to my hotel I met Mr. ——— , and returned with him to his house, when amidst much laughter on all sides, I was introduced to his wife, who proved to be the lady who had opened the door, and I spent a very pleasant evening with these hospitable people.

The next morning I took the stage to Shadiac, and from thence travelled by train to St. John, where my appearance and get up was the cause of considerable chaff from my brother officers.

I shall here say a few words in answer to those who declare that moose calling is no sport, and is taking an unfair advantage of the animal. The man who makes such a statement, and I have heard and read of several doing so, I put down as belonging to one of three classes. Either he is entirely ignorant except by hearsay of what he is writing or talking about, if so, he must at once be put on one side as unable to judge. Or he is an unsuccessful sportsman, who has failed through want of knowledge of the woods. If such be the case, he has likely enough hired worthless Indians, who humbugged him, and would not, or probably could not, call a moose. Perhaps he has been induced by a good deal of " tall talk " to join a party of five or six settlers, who pretended to know everything, but knew nothing, except how to consume an unlimited supply of rum, and make noise enough to disturb all the animals in the neighbourhood. Under these circumstances the grapes are sour, as the man in question abuses a sport which he is not able to accomplish. Lastly, in the case of those individuals who are of the wrong breed, who feel no excitement or pleasure in sport of any kind, whether it be the hooking of a salmon, shooting a stag, or any of those stirring pursuits that rouse ordinary mortals, Englishmen in particular.

I think sufficient has been written to enable my readers to judge of the excitement of the above-mentioned sport.

As regards its unfairness, it must be conceded that such is not the case, where the animal has many more chances in favour of escape than of falling a prey to the rifle of the hunter.

There are few Indians in these days who can call a moose, and I know from personal experience that it takes a long time to acquire the art, as it was only after several months of practice that I was enabled to imitate the call correctly. "Moose-calling" does not last much longer than a month, during that time on an average not more than one night in five is calm enough. If there is any breeze the animal is sure to approach up-wind, consequently he smells you, and decamps altogether from the neighbourhood. In fact, it does positive harm to go out calling on a windy night, inasmuch as it damages your chance for a favourable one. The slightest noise will probably mar everything. The animal, if you go to your station by land, may come across your track, when he turns back at once. This misfortune happened to me on one occasion, and cannot be guarded against, unless you are able to place yourself in a canoe on a lake or dead-water. Two moose answering from opposite directions, generally results in neither coming up, as they are afraid of one another, though there have been instances of their meeting and fighting it out. When a moose does come within range it is not always so easy to hit him, especially if the night is dark.

In the event of hearing a bull and cow together, it is a good plan to go towards them at early dawn, making the call of the male now and then, and imitating the noise made by horns against the bushes. He will probably advance to meet you, thinking it is another bull coming to fight. In this manner one sometimes gets a shot.

I have seen several attempts to describe in writing the call of the moose, but always without success. I shall not therefore add another to the list of failures.

I would advise anyone going on a moose-calling trip to take plenty of warm clothing, as it is exceedingly cold work sitting out all night without a fire, more especially towards the morning when it is often frosty. Indeed I have felt the cold more on these occasions than in mid-winter with the thermometer at zero.

Undoubtedly the most favourable spot for moose-calling is a chain of lakes, or a long dead-water, provided you have a canoe. By this means tracks are avoided, and the ground is always fresh.

Care must be taken not to make any noise, and even in camp your chopping should be done on a windy day. Apropos of this, there is a story of a former Governor of Nova Scotia who went out with some officers moose-calling. The party was a convivial one, and amused themselves in camp with songs, &c. They had no sport, and on finding fault with the Indian on their want of success, he replied, " You think moose big fool like you to come near when you make so much noise."

Another legitimate way of hunting these animals is stalking, termed—" still hunting " or " creeping." This is comparatively easy with light snow, but early in the fall requires great judgment, consummate skill, and an intimate knowledge of the habits of the animal. The Nova Scotia Indians are the only men I know of who can " creep " moose without snow. October is the best month, the leaves by that time have mostly fallen, and the animals have not cast their horns.

The following is the manner in which creeping is carried on.—Having found moose tracks, fresh browsing, or other signs, which indicate the presence of the animal in the vicinity, the Indian leaves the track and keeping to leeward makes a circuit which he narrows until he again comes upon the trail, when he strikes off as before. This plan is repeated until he sees the animal or starts him without doing so, which sometimes happens.

The reason for not following the track, even supposing it points up-wind, is, that the moose when he lies down always turns on one side and goes down wind, so in the event of any enemy following, he would by his smell be aware of the danger before it was too late.

If the ground is unfavourable for tracking, the direction of the animal when feeding is indicated by the manner in which the young shoots, he has been browsing on, are bitten off. The moose severs the twigs by an upward movement of the jaw, which leaves the stump of the twig longer on the nearer than on the reverse side. A person breaking off a few shoots can easily demonstrate this. By scraping away the outer bark of a twig just below where it has been severed, you can tell by the colour of the inner bark at what period of the year the animal was there.

Although the power of smell in the moose is not so acute as that of the cariboo, their sight and hearing is exceedingly quick. The greatest caution is therefore necessary when stalking them. One false step on a dry stick may ruin all. Moose may be killed in the summer months in lakes and dead-waters, either by waiting near their roads, or when feeding, out of a canoe. In hot weather they plunge themselves into the water, generally towards evening, to escape the flies and feed on the roots of water lilies and other aquatic plants. The animal keeps his head some time under water pulling up roots ; if in a canoe, you then paddle as hard as you can, and stopping as soon as he raises his head, remain perfectly still. This plan is repeated until you are near enough to try a shot. It is well known that every animal takes less notice of an object on the water than on land.

Towards the end of February, from the effects of the sun by day and frost by night, a hard crust is formed on the snow, which is generally deep at that time of year. The pot hunters and would-be sportsmen now sally forth. The moose

being started from his yard is followed by the
men on snow shoes, sometimes accompanied by
dogs, who head the animal and bring him to
bay. Even in the absence of dogs he is soon
overtaken, for his sharp pointed hoofs sink into
the snow, and the crust cuts his fetlocks. There
he stands, helpless and unable to escape. The
muff is sure of his prey, as he might fire sixty
rounds at him. In the event of white men
going out with Indians, the latter always out-
strip the former in running; the Indian heads
the moose, and waits until the white man,
exhausted and blown, arrives. He does not
always kill him with the first shot. Sometimes
if the snow is not very deep the moose runs a
good distance before he is overtaken, but cannot
escape when once headed.

I am sorry to say that this abominable and
unsportsmanlike practice is followed by Englishmen calling themselves sportsmen, and in some
instances by British officers, in the neighbourhood
of Quebec, and Ottawa especially. In Nova
Scotia and New Brunswick this species of murder
is confined chiefly to the settlers and Indians,

who have in New Brunswick well nigh exterminated this noble animal.

Moose can be easily tamed, a former Governor
of New Brunswick used to drive a pair in a
sleigh.   They are able to accomplish a very long
journey.

CHAPTER VI.

Salmon rivers of Nova Scotia—Flies in use—The rivers east of Halifax—Scenery of Cape Breton—Description of the settlers—The
Margaree river—Salmon fishing in the St. Laurence tributaries—
American trout—Bass spearing—Advantage of making your own
flies.

THERE are many excellent salmon rivers in Nova
Scotia, but they are much damaged by netting
and spearing, and in some instances altogether
blocked up by impassable mill-dams.

The salmon fishing in this province commences
much earlier than in other parts of North
America, especially in the rivers lying to the
westward of Halifax, where fresh fish can be
taken with a fly in March.

The Indian and Gold rivers, within forty miles
of Halifax, afford fair sport at times, and are the
earliest streams.   In the spring large flies take
in these waters.   Greys, fiery, browns, and the

Nicholson, all of them tied with rather gaudy wings, kill well.

The Le Havre is a splendid stream emptying into the sea at Liverpool; forty miles further to the westward. The bottom of this river is dark, and I found that flies, as gaudy as those used at Ballyshannon, did good execution. Yellow body, yellow hackle, jay shoulder, with a gaudy mixed wing, and a couple of toppings over all, proved an excellent fly in high water. Since I visited this stream it has been totally destroyed by the erection of an impassable mill-dam at the mouth.

Twenty miles to the west of the Le Havre is Mill river, a capital stream. The fish here are bothered by sawdust, and the angler by lumber driving; however, notwithstanding these drawbacks, fair fishing is sometimes to be had. The same flies as for Le Havre suit this river, also the " Admiral," a fly of repute in many parts of the country, but with which I never yet succeeded in raising a fish, although I tried it in various places. To the east of Halifax the salmon run later. The best river on that coast is the St. Mary's, but it is so horribly poached and

speared, that any sport is a great uncertainty.
The same class of flies as those mentioned above
are used in this river. There are many other
smaller streams, where, occasionally, after a
freshet, fish may be killed.

I paid a visit one summer with a brother
officer of the name of Farquharson, to the Margaree, a river of Cape Breton. We travelled
from Pictov by steamer, to Port Hawksbury ;
from thence by land to the Bras d'or Lake, an
immense inland sea connected with the salt
water by very narrow straits. We crossed this
lake by steamer to Bedeque, and drove from that
place to the valley of the Margaree, distant
twenty-seven miles.

We brought a canoe with us from Halifax,
together with an Indian, who proved but a bad
hand at poling, and was altogether a poor specimen of his race. Our driver, who started from
Bedeque elated, got more drink on the road,
and ended by nearly capsizing us down a preci-
pice. After we reached our destination, this
man having only rested his horses an hour, and
still exceedingly intoxicated, set out to drive
home, on a pitch-dark night. They get their

worth out of horses in North America, though
the animals are rarely sound from being over-
worked when young.

Cape Breton boasts of some very pretty scenery,
the valley of the Margaree, in particular. The
river, for the first twenty miles from its mouth,
runs through broad "interval" land, backed
by high and steep hills covered with forest.
"Interval" is the word used to denote meadow
land on the banks of rivers, which are covered
by the spring floods. This alluvial soil is very
valuable, and produces large crops of hay.

The settlers here were a peculiar set of people,
almost all Highland Scotch and Roman Catholics, speaking Gallic in addition to English, some
even not knowing the latter language. I met a
Scotch wǒman nearly a hundred years old, who
had been all through the Peninsular war with
her husband, a soldier in a Highland regiment.
These people were most kind and hospitable, but
some of them very ignorant, and rather lawless.
As an instance of their ignorance, we were actually asked by a well-to-do settler, if it was true
the Duke of Wellington was dead, and if he was
not a great general!

The poaching on the Margaree is far worse than in any other river in North America, the settlers spearing and netting the pools nightly, in open defiance of the law. We were much annoyed by their spearing the pool opposite our camp, and reported it to the chief warden, who was afraid to do anything, and as the settlers came in gangs of over twenty, with blackened faces, we could not identify them, and so were powerless.

I was informed that the late chief fish-warden was a plucky fellow, who did his duty and prevented poaching to a great extent, but his politics not suiting the Hon. Member for the District, he was turned out to make way for the present useless individual.

The river is naturally most prolific, the fish run over twenty pounds in weight, and rise well. There are no rocks in the lower part of the stream, and the pools are smooth, compared to most American waters. The bottom is gravel and sand, so the salmon "stands" vary more or less with the spring freshets, new pools being formed and old ones silted up or changed. Among the best fishing stations are the Forks, and the Island pool, half a mile lower down.

I cared less for the Margaree than any
river I had ever visited in North America. It
was too civilised, and you were apt to have your
camp surrounded, especially on Sundays, by a
crowd of loafers and gaping natives. One after-
noon, whilst making flies in camp and resting
the river for the evening cast, I was horrified at
the sight of two tourists in Rob Roy canoes,
splashing about in the middle of our best pool.
They had come down the stream, to the head of
which they portaged their cockney crafts in
carts, after crossing the Bras d'or Lake, which
they had reached by steamer from Halifax. It
is a consolation to know that there are still
plenty of wild rivers, inaccessible to the town
loafer and cock-tail sportsman in a Rob Roy, as
provided he cannot get above you, there is no
fear of his coming up stream, which it would be
impossible to do in such a craft. As a matter of
course, we asked these unwelcome spoilers of our
best cast to partake of the usual camp hospitality. They proved very harmless men, and
only damaged our fishing through ignorance.

The flies I found most killing in the Margaree
were, the old " Nicholson," and a yellow fly, and

when the water was low a fly perfectly black, with
the exception of wood duck in the wing.   Broad
silver tinsel or twist suits this water best.

There is a good marble quarry near the bank
of the river, but it is not worked.   Gold is now
found in one of the tributaries of the Margaree,
and an American company have commenced
working it.   I found some good specimens of
quartz in some high barrens several miles back
from the river, where I spent a couple of days
looking for cariboo, but only saw a few tracks.
The sand flies were here in swarms, while down
in the open intervals there were hardly any flies
at all, which was a great comfort.

Without doubt the best salmon fishing in North
America is in the rivers flowing into the St.
Lawrence ; among the small celebrated of which
are the Jacques Cartier near Quebec, several
tributaries of the Saguenay, the Mingan, Moisic
and many others.

The fish commence to run in the St. Lawrence
about the middle of June.   The same flies as
used in the New Brunswick rivers answer for
these waters ; in the Moisic a fly entirely green
kills at times.   The Nicholson is also good,

and orange bodies with claret hackles ; wings
should not be very gaudy.   Most of these rivers
are rented by Canadians and others.   There is
a good river near Gaspe at the entrance of the
bay of Chaleurs, which is hired by a Canadian.

Sea trout frequent more or less all the rivers
in North America.   In some streams they are
so numerous at the commencement of the
run as to be a positive nuisance to the salmon
fisher.

These fish are not the same species as the sea
(commonly called white) trout of the English
and Irish coasts ; they are a shorter and thicker
fish, more spotted on the back, and with a
yellowish tinge on the belly.   Nor do they jump
out of the water when hooked, like the fish met
with in Connemara and other parts of Ireland.
As to flies they take almost anything, and are
excellent eating.

In most of the rivers there is an enormous
run of gaspereav, a species of herring; they ascend
the fresh water in May, and are caught in
thousands by weirs made of brush, and constructed
in the shape of the letter V with a kind of trap
at the top.   They are also captured at the foot

of heavy falls by dip nets ; a man stands on a platform or rock, and keeps dipping his net into the foam.

These fish are then salted and packed in barrels ; they are soft, without much flavour, and very inferior to the regular herring, which also is taken in large numbers in the Bay of Fundy. The herrings do not appear until after they have dropped their roe, and are not to be compared to the same species that frequent the English coasts.

The shad, an excellent fish, likewise belonging to the herring tribe, and weighing from one to four pounds, ascends the fresh water, but not until June. They are chiefly killed by nets and spears.

Smelts are very plentiful, especially in the St. John river, though they are never sold in the market, being small, and quantity not quality is the first desideratum in this country. At Fredericton our men used to catch hundreds of them with a rod and line. The smelts are quite equal in flavour and superior in size to those caught in England.

I never saw a shrimp in the country. They

would be considered much too small fry, though
a regiment formerly stationed at St. John had
a shrimp net, and some of the officers used
to go out shrimping in the harbour and catch
plenty of them. Of lobsters, as I have before
mentioned, their name is legion.

Many English fish, such as soles, whiting, red
mullet and others do not frequent these coasts.
There are numbers of white bass and sturgeon in
many of the large rivers. The St. John river,
New Brunswick, contains fish of either kind.
We used to have good sport near Fredericton,
spearing bass when they made their appearance
in the early spring. At that time of year they
come to the top of the water in shoals, and play
about for a few minutes at a time.

Two men in a canoe station themselves near
where the bass are playing, and on a shoal coming
to the surface, they immediately paddle as quickly
as possible up to the spot and throw a spear, the
head of which on striking a fish comes out of
the socket, and is held to the pole only by a cord.
This is to enable the fish to play, as they would
otherwise very likely break the hold.

Most of the inland lakes of North America

contain brown trout, which vary in size, appearance and flavour according to the nature of the country where the lakes are situated. Some fish are exceedingly well fed, and of a deep orange colour when cut open, of others the flesh is white and tasteless. The trout vary in size from a quarter to three or four pounds, but generally do not exceed two pounds, and in some waters one pound.

I have generally observed that rocky bottomed lakes contain small and poor fish, whilst those situated in rich and loamy soil the reverse. The trout in lakes which have not been much fished rise greedily. In the neighbourhood of Halifax and other large towns they are much more shy.

I remember when camped on the Nepisiguit lakes the trout rose to every cast, and on bringing a fish into the side of the canoe, he was frequently followed by others eager to take the fly from him. Many times the original fish having wriggled off close to the canoe, the one " in waiting" rose at once and took the fly. I am speaking now of waters that had rarely ever had a fly cast into them.

The trout flies used in lakes are not large, and of almost any shade and pattern.

It is an immense advantage in this country to be able to tie your own flies ; good ones are hardly to be got, except a few imported from home.   As a rule you pay enormously for a very inferior article, both as regards workmanship, material and pattern.   Most of the feathers are dyed, and the hooks weak and bad.

Fortunately for myself I mastered the art of fly-tying years ago, and was therefore independent of the scamped rubbish sold by the tackle makers, more especially those of Halifax.   In St. John, New Brunswick, there was a very respectable, man of the name of Willis —a saw-filer—who could put a decent fly together if he had the materials.

CHAPTER VII.

Small game shooting—Characteristic story of a farmer—Various kinds
of game found in North America—Concerning woodcocks and
where they resort—War-office wisdom—Duck and wild goose
shooting in the St. John river.

THE small game shooting of Canada is indifferent, the only birds that give any sport are
snipe, ducks, geese, woodcock, wild turkey and
quail, the two last mentioned birds are met with
in some of the western parts of Upper Canada,
yet are never found in the Maritime provinces.
The tree grouse show no sport at all, neither do
the hares.

The American woodcock (*scolopax minor*) is
by far the most sporting bird of the whole number.
It breeds in the country, and is much smaller
than the European species, weighing rarely more
than eight ounces. The plumage is also different,
being of a lighter shade on the back, and of a

light yellowish brown on the breast. These birds frequent coverts of alder and young growth of tamarac. Such coverts are chiefly found in the neighbourhood of settlements, on the borders of "intervals," or often in places where the land has been cleared of its forest growth, and then abandoned. The nature of the land has also a good deal to do with the locality in which they are met with ; they prefer black and loamy soil in the neighbourhood of marshes or wet land.

Some large tracts of alder covert which appear in the distance, most likely woodcock ground, prove on close inspection and trial to contain not a single bird. The soil is either unsuitable or the grass is too long. Many a time when exploring new country have I been deceived in this manner, and had a long walk for nothing. Good woodcock coverts are scarce, consequently, sportsmen who know of them keep them dark, and are chary of giving information to outsiders.

In Canada there is an absence of the sporting ruffian frequently to be met with in the garrison towns of Ireland, who knows the whereabouts of every snipe in the neighbourhood. At Halifax

there was a useless impostor—a white man—who
pretended to know everything connected with the
sports of the country, but who in reality was not
even worth his keep in the woods.   This individual once fired at a stuffed moose's head purposely
placed for him in the woods near Halifax—
imagining that it was a living animal.

Woodcock shooting commences on the 1st of
September, but the birds are not fully grown
until October, by that time also the leaves have
fallen, and better sport can be had.   By the end
of that month they have all migrated.   When
quartered at St. John I killed one year forty-four
and a half brace of woodcock from the 1st to the
25th of October.

Good spaniels are indispensable for this shooting, as the birds lie very close ; on rising they
make a low whistling note, and do not as a rule
fly any great distance.   I picked up a spaniel
when a puppy on my first arrival in the country,
and a capital dog he turned out; his name was
" Musquash," the Indian for musk-rat.

A curious fact in this country is the extreme
ignorance of the settlers with respect to natural
history, hardly one knows what a woodcock is

like. If you ask any of the people if they have
seen any about, they invariably imagine you mean
wood-peckers, a species of which the great black
red crested wood-pecker (*picus erythrocephalus*)
is commonly called the cock of the woods.

On one occasion I produced a woodcock out of
my pocket, and asked a farmer, who had replied
as usual to my queries, if he knew what that bird
was. He answered he did not, but had seen such
birds when driving his cows from among the
alders—guessed it must be a snipe, and, added
he, in accents of contempt, " Why don't you
go and shoot partridge ?"—meaning the ruffled
grouse—" it would take many of them things to
make a meal." He could not understand the difference in the sport ; the man also observed,
" They must be pretty hard to kill, as they would
take a deal of seeing on the ground." I replied I
shot them flying. " Well do you now ? I reckon
you must be a ' boss ' gunner to do that, as they fly
mighty fast."

There are a good many snipe in many parts of
North America. In New Brunswick the best
place for snipe shooting is the Tantamar marshes.
They are also numerous in Prince Edward's

island, where there are plenty of woodcock and wild fowl, but no big game.

There are three species of grouse in Canada, erroneously called by the settlers partridges. Their proper names are the ruffled grouse (*tetrao umbellus*), the Canada (*tetrao Canadensis*), the willow (*tetrao albus.*) The two former kind are common, and are found all over the woods, the latter is rare ; I never saw but one bird. They all invariably fly up into the trees on being flushed, where I have killed them with a stone. The Canada species is particularly tame, and can be snared when perched with a long stick and a bit of string. The ruffled grouse are very good eating, but rather dry ; the Canada has a strong flavour of the fir tree, but are eatable when one is hungry.

There is a species of hare (*lepus Americanus*) mis-called a rabbit, which is numerous, but hardly eatable, as they feed altogether on the shoots of the fir trees. In winter they turn white.

Though the settlers are so ignorant of the natural history of the country in which they have been born and bred, they are far from stupid, and in many respects are more intelligent than the same class in the old country. Every man can handle an axe, mend his waggon and build his own " sled "—a kind of rough sleigh, for hauling timber and other heavy stuff. Most of the settlers on the sea or on large rivers can build their own boats.

Apropos of sleds; this reminds me of gun carriages sent out for use in the snow from England at the time of the Trent affair. These machines—I can call them nothing else—were most expensively constructed of the best English oak, bolted and secured with iron in all directions, but warranted to stick fast in the snow without the additional weight of a gun. The runners nearly formed a half circle, and were of solid oak converging inwards, which threw the snow between them, and having so small a portion of their length resting on the ground that they sank down, and all progress was impossible. These useless and expensive articles were with difficulty hauled as far as the St. John Barracks, where they remained, and are probably there to this day. One more added to the many instances of War Office wisdom ! Thousands of country sleds, fit to transport the heaviest guns could have been bought in a week, thus saving a great and useless outlay.

In the Maritime provinces of Canada the duck shooting is not of much account, for although in places a good many birds are sometimes killed, there is so much water and feeding ground, and so few reeds and rushes, that though seeing plenty of ducks it is hard to get near them.

In New Brunswick the St. John river, from the many lakes, creeks and marshes connected with it, is the headquarters of the wild fowl. This river is the largest in the province, and is navigable by good sized steamers, as far as Fredericton, up to which point the stream is sluggish ; smaller boats go up to Woodstock, seventy miles further.

Plenty of salmon are caught in the tide-way with nets, but of course the absence of a swift current and the great depth of the river precludes fly fishing. The expanse of water is also too great, being over a mile wide in some places, and in parts intersected by large islands, producing great crops of hay.

High up in the numerous tributaries the water is rapid, but the fish there are few and far between. With the exception of the Nashwauk, now blocked by a mill-dam, and the Tobique, I never heard of salmon being taken with a fly in the St John waters. In the Nashwauk, which empties itself into the main stream at Fredericton, there are plenty of lamprey eels, but the natives will not touch them.

The barracks at Fredericton are charmingly situated within twenty yards of the St. John river; a smooth lawn lies in front surrounded by fine old willows. When stationed there I used to get pretty fair sport, flight shooting in the Duggaway, a swamp fifty miles below Fredericton.

Steam boats, two of which came up and down the river daily, afforded great facilities for shooting all down the stream.

I generally took a canoe on board, and was dropt wherever I wished ; spending two or three days in one place, and camping out on one of the islands. In this manner, often accompanied by a brother officer of the name of Grant, I had many pleasant days shooting.

I always made it a rule never to put up at a house if it was possible to camp, as one is so much more independent and comfortable in the latter case, besides being more ready for an early start in the morning.

In the spring of the year, when the ice is breaking up, there are large flocks of wild geese in Grand Lake, St. John river. These are killed by making a blind with blocks of ice, behind which the sportsman sits. Decoys, viz., wooden geese, being placed on the ice within shot. On the approach of geese, their call is imitated, generally by an Indian hired for the purpose. The geese hearing the call and seeing the decoys, circle round within shot. Ducks are also killed with the aid of decoys, which are anchored in the water within convenient distance of your canoe, which is hidden by bushes or rushes.

One of the best places for duck and geese shooting in the Maritime provinces is at Point Miscoe.

In Western Canada, in the neighbourhood of London and Hamilton, there is good duck shooting on the rice lakes, where canoes made of bass wood, beautifully built, very light and shaped like a birch bark, are used.

The black duck (*anas stelleri*) is the most com-

mon species in North America, and takes the place
of the mallard at home.   There are also several
other kinds, including teal and widgeon.   The
rarest and most beautiful of its species is the
American wood duck, (*anas sponsa*).   These
lovely birds inhabit shady ponds and creeks in
the woods, and both perch and build in trees.   I
remember in a wood bound creek off the St. John
river, an old birch tree overhanging the water,
in the branches of which, on a hot day in September, I always found some of these birds sitting,
and often shot one.

Bitterns are very common in the marshes ;
they make excellent soup in the month of September, and the feathers are also useful for flies.
There are no landrails in North America, and in
the early summer evenings you rather miss their
harsh note.   Stone plover are sometimes found
in marshes near the sea, I never saw any inland.

Flocks of wild pigeons, pretty birds with long
tails, make their appearance early in the fall ;
they are often met with in fields of buck wheat,
on which they are fond of feeding.   These birds
are smaller than the common English wood
pigeon and are not nearly so numerous as they
were some twenty years ago.

By the end of October all migratory birds
have departed, and these form the majority in
those latitudes. During the winter none remain
but the owls, the grouse, some of the wood-
peckers and the cat-bird, (*turdus lividus*,) commonly known as the moose bird, the Canadian
jay, and a few other minor species.

In November ice begins to form in the rivers,
which are finally frozen up by the end of the
month. Snow falls in November, but rarely remains; from the beginning of December there is
generally snow enough in the woods for hunting
purposes.

CHAPTER VIII.

Cariboo hunting—Description of cariboo—Food and habits of cariboo
—Description of a hunting toboggin—Start on a hunting expedition—The lumber trade—A lumber camp—Mode of life of a lumberer—Dangers and difficulties of the trade—A night in a lumber camp—A fatiguing journey—A camp on fire—Our sport
spoiled by the wolves—Provisions fail—Musk rats as food—Priva-
tions endured on our return home—How we spent Christmas Day
at Cain's river—Return to Fredericton.

EARLY in December is the best time to proceed
on a winter hunting expedition after cariboo.
At this season the skins of the fur bearing animals
are in the best order ; and the rivers, lakes and
marshy barrens are frozen hard.

The cariboo, or North American rein-deer,
(*cervus tarandus*) is found in many parts of
North America.   In Lower Canada it chiefly
frequents the country bordering on the St. Laurence, and is met with in the Maritime provinces,
especially in New Brunswick.

This animal differs in many respects from the
European species, particularly as regards the
horns, which are stouter and in general grow
straighter than those of the European reindeer.
The horns of the cariboo are partially palmated,
and smooth on the surface ; their shape is most
eccentric, no two pair ever being alike.   A full
grown stag weighs over three hundred weight,
and is about four feet in height; the head is full
shaped, with none of the fineness of the red deer
about it ; the neck is very thick ; the legs are
beautifully fine ; the hoofs large, round and split,
which enables the animal to traverse the snow
without sinking.   The does are smaller and rather
finer about the head.   Cariboo vary in colour
according to their age and the season of the
year.   In summer the stags are brown, and the
does nearly black, while in winter they assume a
much lighter shade, resembling somewhat that of
an old donkey.   Very old beasts, whether doe or
stag, are at all times of a still lighter hue.   The
big stags drop their horns in November, the
smaller ones later ; the females, whose antlers
are small but prettily shaped, not until May.

Cariboo feed chiefly on the white moss, (*cla-*

donica rangiferina) also on lichen, and the moss that hangs in festoons from the firs and tamaracs. In summer they will browse on leaves. During winter when the snow is deep, they dig down several feet with their hoofs to get at the white moss, and not with their horns,—long since cast,—as has been erroneously stated.

On one occasion when hunting near the head waters of the Washademoak, I stalked some cariboo, on a very still day, and when there was a bad crust on the snow, which made a crackling with every step. The snow was deep, and the animals, who were hard at work digging for moss, made so much noise with their hoofs, that I was enabled to approach unheard.

In summer time the old stags are solitary. The does are accompanied by their fawns, and sometimes by young stags. At the approach of the rutting season in September, cariboo congregate in herds, each of which has a master stag, who fights all interlopers.

When winter sets in, the big stags herd together, the small stags still remaining with the does. The principal resort of these animals is in the neighbourhood of barrens, or in open

7

woods of scrubby spruce or pitch pine, where grows the white moss, their favourite food. There are large tracts in New Brunswick answering to this description ; though in the absence of fir growth they are frequently found in hard wood ridges, but from the comparative scarcity of food in such places, they are never in such good condition as when found in the vicinity of barrens.

Cariboo never remain stationary in one place like moose, but are always wandering about from plain to plain, revisiting the same spots at intervals. No one, therefore, need be disheartened when hunting these animals, at not seeing fresh tracks, provided there be old ones, as the herds are almost sure to come round again sooner or later. Their meat is excellent, and when fat, surpasses any other venison. The skins make capital rugs and sleigh robes, and when tanned, the leather is exceedingly close in the grain, and very strong. The skins of the old stags killed in the autumn are often beautifully soft and furry. The shanks make good mocassins, as well as hunting pouches, knife sheaths, &c.

Cariboo can be called in the rutting season,

but not in the same manner as moose. The
females do not, as far as I know or can ascertain,
call the males ; but a solitary stag when looking
for does in the rutting season, will come to the
noise made by a stag, for the purpose of fighting
him, as at that time they are most pugnacious.
As an instance, on one occasion when calling moose,
a large cariboo stag came out of the woods making a snorting noise ; this, Sebattis, our Indian,
imitated on his horn, when the animal came
right up to us, giving vent to a gruff kind of
grunt and pawing the earth. He was immediately dropped by a ball from Farquharson's rifle,
a brother officer who was with me.

There have been instances in which cariboo
have been tamed like the Norwegian reindeer.
I once knew an Indian who drove one in a small
sleigh. This animal was eventually bought by
an Englishman.

It is, of course, far better sport to hunt cariboo in the autumn, when the horns are at their
prime, than in winter, when the large stags have
dropped them ; but there is great difficulty in
most parts of Canada in finding the animal during
the fall. For at that time of year the barrens

are in many places wet and swampy, and the cariboo generally only hang about the edges, and are mostly hid in thick woods, where it is impossible to track them.

I certainly did, on several occasions, by chance, kill an odd stag early in the autumn ; but expeditions at this season of the year almost always prove abortive as regards cariboo, for the reasons above stated.

It is better, therefore, to call moose in September, spend October in woodcock shooting, or moose creeping, and wait until the snow falls, and the ice forms, to hunt cariboo.

At the end of November, 1864, Farquharson and myself arranged to proceed on a hunting expedition to the head of the Little South West Mirimichi. This ground was a long way off, and rather difficult of access, but affording the inducement of beaver and other trapping, in addition to shooting cariboo. We hired two Indians, Sebattis, the man I frequently employed, and Joe Bear, son of old Loui Bear, the most famous of the Milicite hunters, now gone to the "happy hunting grounds." We also got together our hunting gear, including four "toboggins."

A hunting toboggin is six feet long, composed of two side pieces of spruce, six inches wide, and one inch in thickness, rounded off in front, and square behind ; these are placed parallel to each other, at the distance of two feet, and joined at the upper sides by wooden benches of maple or other hard wood. Strips of thin sheet iron, two inches wide, and turned up in front to serve as runners, are then nailed or screwed to the bottom of the side pieces ; thin pieces of wood are placed over the benches, on the top of which the load is fastened by ropes, or thongs of hide. It is a good plan to have rings in the side pieces to which your lashings are fastened. In lieu of iron runners cedar may be used, turned up at the ends. Iron runners are better in a thaw, and wooden when the snow is dry. A rope, or better still, a "lugging-strap," is made fast to each side of the foremost benches, the centre of the strap is then put across the chest, and placing your hands behind, you grasp it with a twist, which gives additional purchase. In this manner a man can haul a couple of hundred weight.

Starting from Fredericton, we drove to Boistown, on the Mirimichi, a distance of fifty miles.

On arriving there we found the river still open,
though large quanties of ice were floating down.
Hiring a couple of settlers and their dug-outs,
we poled to the mouth of Rocky brook, ten
miles up stream. From this point we intended
to leave the river, and take to the woods, which
were quite devoid of settlements. Here we fortunately overtook a party of "lumberers,"—men
employed in the cutting of timber,—who were
about to set out in our direction with a sled
and team of horses for their camp, distant fifteen
miles.

There was not any snow on the ground, between the river and the green woods, which were
three miles off; we therefore arranged with
the lumber party to haul all our gear to their
camp, where we arrived late in the evening,
tired and glad to sit down and smoke our pipes
opposite the fire, waiting until the cook had got
ready the evening meal.

I will here endeavour to give a short description of a lumber camp, and how the business is
carried on. The camp is an oblong structure,
built of spruce or fir logs notched at the ends,
so as to fit into each other, the chinks are stuffed

up with moss ; the roof which slopes on each side from the centre, is composed of rough boards, split with an axe from cedar or pine, these are termed " splints." There is a door at one end, and the roof over the fire place, which is situated in the centre of the camp, is left open.

In case the camp is made single, that is to say, with a roof sloping only one way, the fire is placed on one side against the centre of the wall. Round the smoke hole, which is large and wide, boards are sometimes built up a few feet to make a draft and serve as a chimney ; a smoky camp is an abomination, and occasionally met with. The fire place consists of stone dogs, and if placed against the side of the camp, stones or pieces of rock are piled up to prevent the camp from catching fire.

In front of the fire on one side, and running the whole length of the camp, is a bench, hewn out of spruce or fir ; this bench is termed the " deacon seat ; " behind it the men sleep in a row, on fir boughs, with one long rug under and another over them. Two bunks are made at right angles to the fire ; one of these is occupied by the teamster, who has charge of the horses, and is therefore enabled to get up and feed them without disturbing the other men ; the other by the "boss," as the head man is designated.

The cook sleeps on the other side the fire, which it is his duty to keep going all night. On that side he has all his cooking apparatus, consisting of a couple of frying pans, baking oven, kettle and large iron pot, besides numerous tin plates and dishes, knives, &c. It is also part of his work to cut all the fire wood for the camp, and woe to him if he has not the meals ready at the proper time, or does not keep up a fire.

The men breakfast in winter an hour before daylight ; dinner is served at twelve, supper at dark, and a fourth meal later if they wish. Their wages vary from twelve to sixteen dollars per month, and found ; not much either, considering the hard work.

A crew of lumberers have different occupations assigned to them ; the "fellers," who cut down the trees and trim them ; the "swampers," who "swamp"—cut roads—to the felled trees, to enable the "teamster" and his assistants to haul them on a "Bob sled"—two sleds working inde-

pendently and joined with chains—to the banks
of the river or brook where the lumber is " yarded"
—piled up,—ready to be launched into the water
in the spring, when the melted snow transforms
the now insignificant little stream into a raging
torrent.

It requires a large crew of men to pilot this
floating timber down the streams, as many logs
get stuck in trees and stumps ; " hung up" is the
local term applied to these stoppages.   Sometimes
" jams " occur, the logs being piled up one above
another to a great height.   To break a jam and
cut the log which holds the pile together requires
skill, and is attended with considerable danger,
as directly the key log is severed the jam gives
way at once, some pieces of timber shooting up
their ends high out of the water.   The man on
the jam has to get ashore quickly, jumping often
from one floating log to another.   To prevent
him slipping he has spikes in his shoes.

Some of these fellows are surprisingly active,
and will cross a river full of floating trees in
this manner ; no easy feat, as a floating log when
stepped upon immediately turns round and upsets
you at once if you are not very quick.   This

river work is called " stream driving," and the
floating timber the " drive." It is hard and
killing labour ; the men are always more or less
in the water, which is very cold from the melting
snow.   Few can stand it long, and this no doubt
coupled with the extreme dryness of the air, is
one of the causes why consumption is so prevalent
in North America.

The wages during the driving are higher than
at other times, the men working at the head of
the " drive " earn more than those at the tail,
where there are no jams, the smartest men
therefore go in front.   The work at this season
continues from daylight till dark, and five meals
a day are provided.   Temporary camps are made
along the banks, as the drive progresses down
the stream.   When the timber has been driven
down to large rivers or lakes it is rafted, then
wharped, or towed by steamers to the saw mills,
with the exception of what is called " square
timber," or that used for masts and yards, which
is shipped in its present state.

Nothing can exceed the hospitality and kindness of the lumberers, and no man need starve
in the vicinity of their camps.   To offer payment

for food and a night's lodging is quite out of the question, and would be considered an insult. A bottle of rum and drinks round is not refused, or if hunting in the neighbourhood, a quarter of venison is accepted.

But to continue : after we had supped, and all hands were in camp, we were cross questioned in the usual manner relative to where we came from, and where we were going to hunt, our guns minutely examined, and passed round from one to another with the remarks, " Well now," " And what would she cost ? " " I guess that is a complete gun and no mistake," or alluding to our breechloaders which more especially excited their curiosity, " That beats all," with other quaint expressions.

One or two of the men professed to know of places swarming with cariboo and moose. " Any amount of them " near such a brook, " The whole place alive with cariboo, which were that thick that their horns looked like a forest of trees," such a part of the country " beaten solid with moose tracks," and so-forth. Of course none of these stories were to be relied upon for a moment. The knowledge of these people with a few ex-

ceptions is confined to the trees ; as a rule, oddly
enough, they know little of the animals, though
spending half the year in the woods. A grove,
or as they would call it, a "bunch" of pine or
spruce, catches their eyes sooner than the signs
left by a wild animal.

A stray herd of three or four cariboo hanging
about any spot, of course make many tracks,
which to lumberers convey the idea of hundreds
of animals. I do not think their wild stories
are told for the purpose of misleading you, but
more from the habitual practice of exaggeration
in these men, who are always ready to further
your sport if they can, and help you out of any
difficulty. Many is the time when tired and
hungry I have met with a hearty and most
acceptable welcome at their camps.

Having smoked sundry pipes and done a good
deal of talking, we turned in for the night,
Farquharson among the men. I had already
experienced sleeping with a dozen men under
one blanket, packed like herrings. It is a case
of one turn, all turn ; nor is it pleasant to awake
with one man's elbow in your eye, and the knee
of another in your ribs. So with a bag of flour

for a pillow, I slept on the deacon seat, which though hard and narrow, afforded me room to turn to the fire when one side got cold.

Indians, when in a lumber camp never talk or make a remark, even at the most glaring yarns. On asking Sebattis the next day what he thought of the stories of the preceding evening, he replied, "Lumber-men all liars, must think us big fools, believe all they say." We were aroused long before daylight by the voice of the "boss" calling, "Now, boys, tumble up." Farquharson had had quite enough of his anything but downy couch, and declared he would not sleep among the men again.

After breakfast having packed our three toboggins, which when loaded, weighed heavy, we left the camp on our way. Farquharson and myself had a toboggin between us, the Indians one each. We followed an old "sable line," built formerly by Joe Bear; a "sable line" is a line of traps set for that animal. The hauling was exceedingly bad from the slight depth of snow and the numerous "windfalls"—fallen trees—which intercepted our way, and over which our toboggins had to be lifted. We only got about five miles that day, and camped at night in an old hunting wigwam.

The next morning we proceeded on our way with the same difficulties, our progress being slower as we stopped to set up and bait the "dead falls"—wooden traps—along the line. On this evening we were not able to reach a camp, of which there were several on our route, but camped in the snow at the bottom of a very steep hill, which we were too tired to face that day. It was some time after dark when we had rigged up a camp with a blanket, cut wood, and cooked our supper.

After two more days hauling, camping where the shades of evening overtook us, we reached a bark wigwam on the Renous lakes. Here we set some traps for otter and one for beaver at a house near. We had performed a hard day's work, and consequently slept soundly. During the night our camp, which was of birch bark, caught fire, and the consequences might have been serious had not Joe Bear happened to awake, and rousing us up we managed to put it out.

The next morning Farquharson and Joe, leaving one toboggin behind, followed a fresh bear track.

It was just the time of year that these animals were looking out for their winter habitations, so afforded a good chance to get him, provided they found him in his den.

Sebattis and myself taking a toboggin apiece agreed to meet our companions at a camp on the Little South West lake, our ultimate destination, which was only a day's journey from the Renous lakes. We had a very hilly country to traverse, principally of hard wood growth, and what with setting up traps and building a few fresh ones at likely places where the old traps wanted replenishing, it was almost dark when we emerged on to a lake separated from the large lake by a strip of woods half a mile wide. Up to this time we had followed the line which was delineated by the " blazes,"—marks in the trees about the size of a man's hand, where the bark has been cut off.

As Sebattis was a stranger to this part of the country, we had great difficulty, owing to the now increasing darkness, in picking up the line of blazes at the further end of the lake. At length we found it, and entered the woods, which were of spruce growth and exceedingly thick. Our

toboggins caught in the bushes, and upset. We
had frequent falls and much difficulty in making
our way in the dark. After struggling for more
than an hour amongst thick under growth and
many wind-falls, we eventually, to our great relief, emerged on to the lake, which was five miles
long, and half a mile wide, with several islands
interspersed. On one of these Joe had told us
his camp was situated, but how to find it in the
dark was the difficulty.

In a short time the report of a gun was heard,
which I answered, and we soon met our companions, who had come to look for us. They
had reached the camp some hours before, and
seeing nothing of us, as evening approached,
concluded we had missed the way. Inasmuch as
we had all the provisions, it was a bad look out
for them. Farquharson had not succeeded in
getting a shot at the bear, though they came
upon his newly made den.

We had now travelled a distance of thirty
miles from the lumber camp, and had a line of
dead-falls set nearly all the way, with several
steel traps at beaver houses, and likely places
for otters. We had not seen a single track of

either a cariboo or moose ; the former we had
not expected to meet with in the thick woods,
but three years previously moose had been most
plentiful in these regions, until annihilated in
the deep snow by Indians and others, solely for
their skins, as I have before described. This
large tract of wild country, sixty miles from
any habitation, was entirely denuded of those
magnificent animals.

The following morning we left camp at an
early hour, with our rifles and some steel traps,
expecting to find fresh tracks of cariboo, and
perhaps manage to shoot one. The country to
the north of the lake was sparsedly covered with
scrubby spruce and pitch pine, with plenty of
white moss growing everywhere, most likely-
looking cariboo ground.

After a long tramp we were surprised at
seeing none but very old tracks of cariboo,
mingled with those of a pack of wolves, whose
dung we also found to be full of cariboo hair,
thereby proving they had killed and eaten the
game. This accounted at once for the absence
of the deer, and Joe informed us, that when
chased by wolves cariboo do not return to the

8

same ground for a long time—this was indeed a great disappointment.

Having come so far, we decided to make the best of it, and so set to work, trapping vigorously, setting steel traps at three beaver houses in the big lake, and at several others in the many lakes which lay in the surrounding country. We also set traps for otters in several good places, and constructed a new line of about fifty dead-falls across a high hill, near the margin of the lake. It took us two or three days to complete this line, working together, two of us cutting out a path and blazing the line, the others building and baiting the traps. In another place the reader will find the different methods of capturing fur-bearing animals, described under the head of "trapping."

There were some pines growing on a distant ridge, their towering heads being distinguishable a long way off. As yet no lumberers had penetrated to these regions, as from the rocky and rough nature of the rivers, it would be impossible to drive down the timber.

We were now hard pressed for fresh meat, our pork was getting low, and it also turned out

rancid and bad, but it had to be eaten, for we
had as yet caught no beaver. I had observed
some musk-rat houses at one end of the lake, so
sent Sebattis to try and trap some ; he returned
in the evening with three, which we were glad
to get. Musk-rats are not bad eating in winter
time, made into soup, especially if you have no
other meat. We also caught a porcupine, (*hys-
trix dorsata*) which was almost uneatable.

Grouse were very scarce in the neighbourhood.
It is at all times difficult to find them without a
dog in the middle of the forests. We tried to
catch trout through the ice, but without success.
This method of fishing is followed by cutting
holes in the ice and letting down a hook baited
with a piece of pork fat, at which trout often
bite greedily, though it is cold miserable work,
and far from exciting.

The next day our luck seemed to have turned,
for on going round the traps we found three
beavers in them. Another must have had a
narrow escape, as a chip of wood gnawed off by
the beaver had fallen on to the pan, and on the
trap being sprung, flew up and was caught between the jaws, thus enabling him to escape.

At the end of a week, our Indians went round
our more distant traps, Farquharson and myself
remained at the lake, looking after those in its
immediate vicinity. One day we had occasion
to visit a beaver house, and a short line at the
further extremity of the large lake. I never
remember feeling the cold so bitter. A strong
east wind with driving sleet, blew in our faces,
and we had to walk backwards, most of the way.
On reaching the woods, Farquharson was frost-
bitten in the hands, though wearing mits. I had
escaped, but was obliged to change the hand
grasping the barrel of my rifle, every minute.
In the woods it is the practice to carry your gun
on the shoulder, with the muzzle in front for
the sake of balance.

On our return we had not to face the wind,
but the glare ice—from which the slight covering of snow had been blown off—made it very
fatiguing. How I wished we had brought skates.
We did not get back to camp until after dark,
and there was not a stick of wood cut ; luckily
it was moon light, so I set to work to fell trees
and cut them into lengths, which my companion
carried to camp. Joe and Sebattis returned in

a couple of days with a beaver and two sable; they also brought the toboggin which had been left at Renous.

After spending here three weeks, and capturing ten beavers, two otters, a fisher, several sable and mink, we set out on our return. Hardly any snow had fallen since our arrival, so the hauling was still very bad, but the loads were of course lighter, from the consumption of our provisions; Farquharson had cut his leg with an axe, consequently I was obliged to haul a toboggin single handed. The second day we reached a camp on the Dungarvon waters, where we remained a day, and attempted to kill some beaver in a dam, situated on a small brook, by breaking the dam and cutting the ice all round the edges of the pond. After much labour we succeeded in making a gap in the dam, but the ice proving too thick to break up, all our trouble was useless.

On the third day we reached the lumber camp, where we had previously passed the night. The following morning we made an early start, as we had fifteen miles to haul along a lumber road to the mouth of Rocky brook, and a very grievous and

hard fifteen miles it proved. On the advice of
the lumberers we took the brook near their camp,
which was a shorter route, and joined the road
some miles distant. We had not proceeded far
down the ice when it gave way, and Farquharson,
who was in front, fell in. We were obliged
therefore to retrace our steps to the camp, hauling
up a steep hill, and make a fresh start along the
lumber road, which was rough and slippery, being
covered with only six inches of snow, with ice
underneath. This was the result of a rapid thaw
followed by hard frost.

We had not got more than a mile on our
journey when a tremendous snow storm set in,
and before the middle of the day we were plough-
ing through light snow up to our knees. Under
no other circumstances is hauling so heavy; it
was only with immense exertions that we were
able to drag along our toboggins, and the distance
appeared interminable. The road lay over several
very steep hills, the surmounting of which from
the slippery nature of the ground cost us many
falls, nor would snow shoes have mended matters.
At length quite done up we arrived on the banks
of the river at dark, where we made a temporary

camp by sticking up a blanket and clearing away the snow. It proved a miserable place to camp in, being very open and with wood exceedingly scarce. Our supper consisted of a small portion of pork and bread with tea.

The snow storm having cleared off, a bitterly cold night set in. The thermometer, we afterwards discovered, went down to thirty-nine below zero. We were all awoke by the cold, and sat smoking by the fire until morning. A grouse, happening at day break to perch above our heads, was shot by Farquharson with his rifle, and made an addition to our breakfast.

The next day we put on our snow shoes and proceeded down the river on the ice to the settlements, where we arrived in the evening, put up at a farm house, and enjoyed a plentiful meal. Hauling was heavy also on this occasion, but not so bad as on the previous day. The next day a farmer drove us to Cain's river, where we took up our abode in an old lumber camp, hoping to get a shot at a cariboo before our return to Fredericton. No such luck awaited us, for after scouring the country all round, we saw not a single track, although one of the men

at the lumber camp had declared he had seen
plenty in that neighbourhood. As Cain's river
was formerly famous for cariboo, we believed him.
However, Sebattis discovered some moose yarded;
these we determined to creep the first favourable
day when there should be plenty of wind.

We spent Christmas Day at this camp ; our
dinner consisted of pork, beans and bread, with
one bottle of champagne, which we had carried
with us during all our wanderings tied up in a
stocking for this especial occasion.

The following day being windy and the snow
soft, we set out with Sebattis to creep the moose
he had previously discovered. On approaching
the yard we took off our snow shoes, and after
proceeding for about an hour with the greatest
caution, treading in each others tracks as the
snow was now deep, we sighted four moose
about one hundred yards off. Two of the animals
were lying down, the others feeding. Those
lying down immediately became aware of our
approach and jumped up. We fired several shots,
killing one and wounding another, which was
found dead the next day more than a mile from
where he had been struck. The bullets taken

out of the animals proved that we had each shot one, the bore of our guns being different. We did not follow him far the first day, as a badly wounded animal when pressed will run a long distance, but if left alone he lies down, and becoming stiff, is loath to get up again, and probably soon dies. When there is snow, of course it is easy to track him the next morning, unless a heavy storm should intervene and entirely obliterate the track.

It occupied us several days to haul the meat to camp, after which we returned to Fredericton, as our leave was nearly at an end.

CHAPTER IX.

Melancholy death of my Indian guide—Pleasant brook—Exciting
hunt after cariboo—Appearance of the woods in winter—The
Spencer rifle—Comfort of camp after a hard day—Night in camp
—Shoot four bears—Lost in the woods— A silver thaw—The
red deer—Black bears—Concerning some phases of social life in
Canada, as compared with those of England.

DURING the same winter Farquharson and myself
made an expedition to Pleasant brook, a stream
flowing through a tract of country, abounding
in large barrens and much frequented by cariboo.
A few days before setting out on this hunt, I
drove over to the Indian village, fifteen miles
from Fredericton, to see Joe Bear, who was to
accompany us. On inquiry at his house I was
informed that he had not been seen since the
previous evening, when he was in a state bordering on delirium tremens.

I joined a party of Indians who were about to

follow his tracks, which had been discovered leading to the river St. John, on the banks of which the village was situated. From blood and other marks on the snow, it was evident he had fallen down a steep bank on to the ice. Following his trail for some time, which kept on the ice, but in a zig-zag course, we approached a small and well-known air hole which never freezes up, and in size is not much more than twice the diameter of a man's hat. Within a yard of this hole it was apparent by his tracks that he had stood still a short time, and then walked into it, as his footsteps here disappeared.

The body was never found. Poor Joe! I was sorry for him ; he was an excellent hunter, always in a good humour, and the harder the work, the greater the difficulties, the better spirits he was in. He never shirked his work, and was the only Indian I ever met who always paid back any money he borrowed. Many a laugh and jolly evening we have had together in camp, but like many others of his race he could not, when out of the woods, withstand the fire water of the pale faces. This in the end proved his destruction.

We set off for the head of Pleasant brook the end of January with Sebattis and another Indian named Gabe, a well-known hunter at Fredericton, who spoke excellent English, and did not use Yankee terms for everything. This man from his earliest youth had been accustomed to go out with officers stationed in the province.

We drove forty miles from the barracks, and then hauled our luggage on four toboggins fourteen miles into the woods. The country was flat and the snow deep, and moreover our way led across numerous barrens, the hauling therefore was easy enough. We took up our quarters in a double bark camp situated in some "green" woods, a quarter of a mile from a large barren. We had seen several tracks of cariboo on the way thither, and as there was not a sign of wolves, we had great hopes of sport.

It was dark on our arrival at the camp, and it took a considerable time to clear away the snow therein accumulated and get ready our food. On the following day I set off with Sebattis, Farquharson with Gabe, each taking opposite directions. On my return to camp alone—Sebattis having gone off to set some traps for lynx—when crossing a large barren I suddenly saw five cariboo come round a point of woods. The deer were making straight towards me, and as there were no bushes near, I threw myself flat on the snow. The cariboo approached and did not see me in my white blanket coat. The herd was now heading so as to pass within about a hundred yards, a young stag leading. When within about that distance I gave a sharp whistle, on hearing which they stopped, the stag looking intently in my direction ; raising my rifle I fired, a heavy thud followed, as the ball struck, and down came the stag on his haunches. The remainder scampered off, yet halted and looked round after they had gone a hundred yards. I gave the nearest my second barrel, but the bullet flew over him— express rifles were not much known in those days. Sebattis, who on hearing the shots had turned back, shortly made his appearance. Having skinned the stag and covered him up with snow, we returned to camp where my companion had already arrived, having killed one cariboo. We now all set to work to cut fire wood, as there were two hours of daylight left. It is no joke having to do this after a long day, especially in the dark.

It is the invariable habit of cariboo, when started by a shot or otherwise, to stop after running a short distance ; sometimes they make several halts, and thus give the sportsman many chances. The best plan is to run immediately they make off, keeping of course, to leeward and out of sight as much as possible. The moment the animals come to a stand, the hunter should do so likewise. By this means I have often fired several times at the same herd.

There is something singularly fascinating in the American forests in winter. In the morning you go forth from your camp fresh and vigorous for the day's hunting, the keen air bracing you up for any exertion. The sun shines brightly on the glittering snow, and it quite dazzles you to survey carefully a plain in search of game. If there is no wind the stillness is only broken by the sharp tap of a woodpecker—which can be heard at the distance of a mile—the chatter of a moose-bird, or the chirp of a squirrel. At night all is hushed, and nothing breaks the awe-like stillness but the cracking of the trees, which, if the frost is very intense, make a report as loud as that of a pistol.

The next five days we were unsuccessful in getting a shot, though meeting one large herd ; but from the crust on the snow and the absence of wind, we were unable to get within range.

On the sixth day we came across a herd, and I made a lucky shot in some burnt woods, putting a ball through an animal's neck, at two hundred yards. By running a couple of miles we managed to head the herd in a small barren, where Farquharson, who was with me, killed a fat doe, and I wounded another. On this day, for the first and last time, we used Spencer-repeating rifles, and great failures they turned out, for not only did the whole mechanism of the magazine in the heel plate become frozen up, by reason of the lubricating mixture on the cartridges, but after this had been remedied by its removal, the cartridges themselves missed fire, in about the average of five out of six. This was most trying to one's temper, and lost us several good chances. After this miserable performance we discarded these useless weapons, and fell back on our muzzle loaders.

The next morning I set off with Gabe to try and get the cariboo I had wounded the day pre-

vious.   After following its tracks for many miles
without success, we came upon the trail of a
fresh herd, which led us on to a large barren.
Suddenly, when in the midst of it, Gabe fell on
his face in the snow, I followed suit.   There was
the herd lying down within two hundred yards.
Forcing myself along through the snow, I at
length managed to decrease the distance by half,
and fired at a doe with pretty horns.   At the
report of my rifle away went the deer, the doe that
was fired at included.   At this apparent miss I
felt much disgusted ; however, the doe began to
lag behind after running a few hundred yards,
and ultimately staggered and fell dead.

By the time we had skinned the cariboo it was
late in the day.   We had travelled a long distance, and the snow shooing was exceedingly
heavy, as it was thawing, and with every step
you took up pounds of snow ; yet to camp we
must get, although it was about ten miles off.
Fortunately our route lay chiefly through barrens, where there are no fallen trees or brush
wood, to trip one up and cause delay.   Much
fatigued we at length arrived at the barren, near
the end of which, about two miles distant, our

camp was situated. Taking it in turn to break
tracks, we plodded silently on. What an interminable length that barren seemed ; every hundred yards appeared a mile. The woods at the
end of the barren, which in the darkness, looked
at a great distance, never, apparently, became
any nearer. At last weary and worn-out, we
turned into the woods, and soon saw the sparks
of our camp fire through the trees.

The delight of getting to camp after such
fatigue, is known only to those who have experienced it in the woods. Kicking off your snow
shoes, putting on dry socks, and exchanging your
shooting jacket for a loose blanket coat, you eat
a hearty meal, of soup, venison, bread, and perhaps marrow bones, washed down with strong
tea; then reclining on your blankets you enjoy
a pipe, not of bird's eye or shag, but of fragrant
honey dew, mixed with " nespeponkoul,"—willow bark. The perfect repose and comfort of
that smoke cannot be described, nor would I on
such occasion exchange my situation for the best
room in England, and the most cunningly de-
vised arm chair ever produced. If awakened in
the night by the cold, you pile on fresh logs, and

as they blaze up, take a few draws of your pipe,
then turning to the fire you roll yourself in your
blankets and are soon asleep. Gabe proved a
most amusing companion in camp, sang capital
songs, and told excellent hunting stories.

I never take grog out hunting, as when tired
it only stimulates for the time, and you soon feel
more done up than ever ; but on reaching camp
a nip is acceptable. Two pieces of bread, with a
slice of pork between them, was my usual lunch.
On a cold day, this had to be wrapped up and
hidden away in the innermost recesses of my
shirt, or it would soon be frozen as hard as a
brick.

Our camp now presented a sporting appearance, with cariboo hides stretched on frames,
heads and meat hanging in all directions. We
had plenty of good venison, abundance of excellent fire-wood, and fared sumptuously. Very
different to our food on the little South-West
Mirimichi. The usual number of moose-birds
had collected and fed on the meat about the camp,
hopping within a few yards of us. However
much these birds eat, they are always as thin as
herrings. They are soon attracted by blood or

meat, and five minutes after killing an animal you hear them chattering close by ready for their feast.

After three weeks hunting we returned to Fredericton, having killed nine cariboo, all of which we brought in, some of them whole. The venison of the does was fat and in good order.

I made many other expeditions into the woods with varied success. On one occasion when hunting in December, at the head of the Washademoak, I had great luck in meeting with bears. There was only a few inches of snow on the ground, and we were traversing a hard wood ridge, when my attention was drawn by a curious whining noise. Looking about I saw a dark moving mass in a cavity formed by the uprooting of a large tree. "Bears," exclaimed Sebattis, (who accompanied me) in an excited whisper. I immediately let drive both barrels into the lot, Sebattis, quick as lightning, laid about him with his axe on the noses of the cubs, as they attempted to escape through the roots of the tree. On hauling them out, we found an old she bear and three large cubs ; the former had been killed by a lucky shot, and two of the cubs were

hit. Their skins were in first-rate order, and
eventually made a splendid robe. It is a very
rare occurrence to find more than two cubs in a
den.

During this trip I got lost in the woods. I
had left camp very early in the morning, and
toward evening came out on a large plain, where
I fired at, and missed a cariboo. The sun was
nearly down, and my Indian, a man of the name
of Noel Lolah, who was a stranger to this part
of the country, told me our way to camp lay in
a certain direction, which we accordingly took.
I soon discovered that we were astray, and Noel
at length owned he was lost. Visions of roast
venison, &c., in our camp rose up before me,
but where on earth was our camp?

After scrambling several hours in the dark,
through thick woods, we eventually came to a
wild beaver meadow ; out of this I knew there
must be a road leading somewhere, as hay was
cut here every year. In a short time Noel, who
had gone to look for a road, returned, having
found one, which we followed for a long way,
and at length arrived about midnight, quite
done up from fatigue and hunger, at a deserted

lumber camp. I was so tired that I felt as if
I could have lain down and slept in the snow.
We searched the camp carefully for provisions,
but found nothing but a barrel of salt and an
old pair of boots. Having made a good fire we
were obliged to content ourselves with a pipe,
and sleep as best we could, without a blanket or
covering of any kind. We rose with the dawn,
and Noel then discovered that we were twelve
miles from camp, where we arrived about noon,
quite faint from want of food. But a tin of tea
and a cariboo steak soon set us all right. I had
at first tried to stifle my hunger with smoking, but
after a time this lost its effect. I wished I was
able to chew tobacco, as Noel appeared to stave off
his hunger by that means. It was very stupid
and green of him to lose himself in the way he did;
had Sebattis been with me I should have been sup-
ping off cariboo, instead of starving in the woods.
I afterwards discovered that on our making for an
imaginary camp the evening we went astray, we
were in reality only four miles from home, and took
a course at right angles to the proper direction.

On my return from this expedition, in which
we met with very good sport, I witnessed for the

first time a silver thaw in all its beauty—one of
the most lovely sights in North America. The
snow had fallen from the trees and rain set in,
which on the wind chopping round suddenly
from South to North, froze as it fell, covering
every twig and blade of grass, with ice of about
the thickness of a half crown. It was a very
bright moonlight night, and the effect was most
beautiful. We appeared to be in a land of
crystal; the trees, the branches of which were
rigid, shone like diamonds, the firs especially
reared their stiffened heads in unparalleled magnificence, and the scene altogether was one of
fairy-like splendour.

The red deer (*cervus verginianus*) inhabits
many parts of North America, but is more numerous in the Western than in the Maritime
provinces of Canada; it is also found in Maine
and other parts of the United States. This
animal is of a reddish brown color, with coarse
long hair, and in height stands about eight hands;
the head is small, and the nose fine like the
European species. The horns are not large,
though prettily shaped and curved inwards at
the points; the hoof is small and pointed. The

food of the red deer is the same as that of the moose. They frequent lakes in summer and yard in winter after the manner of that animal. With regard to hunting, they cannot be called in the rutting season, but from the shape of their hoofs they are easily run down in deep snow. It is a difficult matter to creep them, for they are more wary than any deer in the country.

In the Western provinces of Upper Canada red deer are hunted with dogs, and when chased they invariably make for the nearest lakes, where the guns are placed near their runs, or at the spots where the deer are likely to take to the water. This is comparatively poor sport to stalking; moreover, one may be a week without ever getting a shot, and there is none of the excitement of creeping up to a wild animal.

In parts of the United States where they are very numerous they are sometimes killed at night, out of a canoe, in the following manner:— The hunter places behind him a pan of blazing pitch pine, and paddles noiselessly along the shores of lakes; he will thus be able to see the eyes of the deer shining, and to get a shot at any animals feeding in the water on roots, or along the shore.

The wapiti, the king of the red deer tribe, inhabits the regions bordering on the Rocky Mountains; it is also found in British Columbia and Vancouver's Island. Of these magnificent animals I cannot speak from personal experience, so shall not attempt to describe either themselves or their habits.

The American black bear (*ursus niger Americanus*) is found in all parts of the country, but it is a mere chance ever getting a shot at one. They keep in thick woods, and make off at the approach of man so quickly that, although their tracks are often met with, the animals are seldom seen. I only saw bears twice during the whole time I was in North America, though I have seen their tracks and other signs many times. The most probable place to get a shot, is on the blueberry plains in autumn, bears being fond of all berries, and blueberries in particular. In one year, during the month of September, when, owing to the drought, there were no berries of any kind, these animals were driven by hunger to the settlements, where they committed depredations on the crops. Some of my brother officers, then stationed at Fredericton, shot several

by waiting of an evening in the corn fields,
where the bears were in the habit of feeding.

Black bears are numerous in Anticosti, where
they may be killed along the seashore, which they
frequent in search of fish.   The American black
bear will seldom attack man, except in the case
of a she-bear, wounded, and defending her cubs.
I have heard stories from Indians that he-bears,
in the rutting season, go about in packs of three
or four ; and if, at that time, they come on a
man's track, they will follow it, and tear him to
pieces should they come upon him.   I have met
Indians who told tales of their having had to run
for their lives under these circumstances.   I cannot vouch for the truth of their stories, though
as I have heard them from different sources, I am
inclined to think they are not altogether untrue.

The wolf (*canis lupus*), is not plentiful in the
Maritime provinces, though met with occasionally, as I found to my cost when at Little Sou'-
west, Mirimichi.   They are pretty numerous in
the more northern regions of Canada, and do not
differ from the European species.

There are game laws in the Dominion of
Canada, but they are for the most part a dead-

letter, and faulty in their construction. The great obstacle in enforcing the laws proceeds from the fact that the county magistrates themselves are frequently the chief violaters of them ; for instance, they destroy moose out of season, setting snares and other poaching and illegal contrivances. Any settler is made a magistrate, and is thereupon designated " Squire," as a distinguishing appellation. These " Squires " are as thick as blueberries all over the country. Many of the station-masters are magistrates, and as there are only about three trains a day, on the New Brunswick and Halifax lines, they have plenty of time to attend to their magisterial business.

With regard to the rail-roads, there is much to amuse and astonish the traveller fresh from the Midland Express or the Limited Mail. The traffic is carried on in an easy-going manner the other side the water. There appears to be an entire absence of all hurry, and time seems no object. I have seen a train kept waiting, to enable the conductor and station-master to have a chat. There are no porters at the stations,— car depots is the local name,—when you drive

up, to seize your gun case with a " Where to,
Sir," a shilling being plainly stamped on their
countenances. The conductor has charge of the
train, under him, the baggage-master and his
assistants. The check system is here in vogue,
and answers very well, especially as there are so
few hands to see to the passengers' luggage.
Once, on asking a railway official a question relative to my luggage, I was told that I had
better apply to " that gentleman," pointing to a
man in his shirt sleeves, who was placing the
baggage in the train. In America every man is
a gentleman, and woman a lady. A friend, with
whom I was travelling on one occasion, on leaving
an hotel, offered the chambermaid a fee, which
was indignantly refused, with the remark—
" American ladies do not take money from English gentlemen."

The conductor is often a great man in his
own estimation, and looks upon the passengers as
so many people who, if they could dodge him,
would avoid paying their fares. At the same time,
although to an Englishman new to the country,
these railway servants appear at first rude and
brusque in their manners, yet, if he only knows

how to manage them, and does not put on "side," they will do all in their power to oblige him. For my own part I have almost invariably received the greatest courtesy; and where I was known to the railway officials, from constant travelling on the line, there was nothing they would not do for my convenience. Under these circumstances, the conductor comes up with a "How are you, Captain," and a shake of the hand, "going gunning, I see." He then takes my dogs, and puts them away in the baggage-van, free of charge. Instead of the "Take your seats, gentlemen," it is "All aboard." Several men, at the last moment, jumping on to the train in motion, as it moves out of the station. This is done without danger of accident, as at the end of each carriage there are platforms. The engine-drivers are sheltered from 'the weather by a snug house, with glass sides and front. Why this is not done at home, I have often wondered. I suppose from the intense obstinacy of the English, and their dislike to adopt any new wrinkle—especially American—which is opposed to the old plan of doing things.

The English in some cases appear particularly

fond of things cumbersome and unwieldy. An
English felling axe is the consummation of a
tool ill-shaped, badly balanced, and worse handled
—the handle is bent the wrong way, and so
adjusted as to destroy the swing and balance
of the axe as much as possible. The head is
also shapeless and clumsy; the only good point
is the steel. I believe that English makers have
at last commenced to manufacture axes on the
American pattern. There is no doubt of one
thing which they have discovered—that no man
on earth except an English countryman will buy
an English axe.

Some years ago a Canadian firm sent to
England for a number of axe heads, sending a
wooden model of the shape required. As the
model had not the hole cut in it for the handle,
the English makers sent out the axes solid without a hole for the handles ! There are many other
articles in America very superior in design and
shape to those of England. For instance, you
see a man in the old country sawing fire wood
with a common hand saw, instead of using a
frame saw, which is twice as effective and requires
much less labour.

It cannot be said that all these improvements are due to the British Colonies, in that they are chiefly borrowed from the States. The colonists themselves, especially of Nova Scotia, a few years ago were pretty much as represented in " Sam Slick," which gives in reality a truthful description of the country, and not at all a caricature, as many readers might suppose.

CHAPTER X.

Camping—Dress for the woods—Personal requisites for a hunting expedition—Particulars of kind and quantity of food necessary for a hunting expedition—Camp—Cooking utensils—Extra necessaries required for winter—Snow shoes—Cooking in camp—Tents and how to pitch them—A "Lean to"—How to build a camp—Manner of curing deer skins—Advice on the construction of traps—How to set a line of traps.

THE best dress for the woods in summer or the fall, is a smock and trousers of grey home-spun, the former loose, with plenty of pockets, and fastened round the waist by a strap, to which is suspended a knife-sheath, and if shooting, a cartridge pouch made of seal skin or deer shanks. A shooting coat is useful on land, but unless made very short, it will be in the way when paddling a canoe. The hat should be grey felt, with broad brim in summer, to enable a veil to be worn, as protection against the flies. Light shooting boots are suitable for fishing, but if poling a canoe, or creeping animals in the fall,

mocassins should be worn, made of tanned cow-
hide, or cariboo shanks. Very thick country-
made socks are the best ; these· are to be had
everywhere for a quarter dollar a pair. They
should be pulled up over the trousers, to prevent
flies from crawling up the legs, and to serve instead of gaiters, which are not required, as there
are no thorns in North America.

The principal requirements of dress in the
woods is a material which is at the same time
light and warm, and above all things dries
quickly. The common homespun of the country
answers all these wants, being made entirely of
wool and loosely woven.

The following are the requisites for a month
in the woods, either for fishing in the summer
or hunting in the fall:—One homespun smock;
one short shooting jacket; three pairs of thick
country socks; two pairs of long stockings; one
pair of thick drawers; a sailor's knitted guernsey
and a pair of mitts for moose calling; three flannel
shirts; two pairs of mocassins; one pair of shooting boots; one waistcoat; one blanket coat of a
grey color with hood; three blankets; one water-
proof coat; one waterproof sheet; a bag made of

shanks or sealskin, sewn with raw hide, lined with flannel, and of the same shape as a cartridge bag, but twice the size. This article no real hunter should be without, and it is called in Indian a "pitsnargan." Into this is packed a crooked knife; awls crooked and straight; bees' wax; cobblers' wax; shoemakers' thread; house-wife; wet stone; file; tacks; oil; tow and rags for guns; Cockle's pills and Diaculon plaster; screw driver; packing needle for stretching beaver skins; small skinning knife; corkscrew and gimlet. I generally carried two pitsnargans, one of bea-ver's skin for ammunition, the other of cariboo shanks for the articles above mentioned, both impervious to wet or damp. In addition should be supplied strong string for stretching hides; soap; towels; dish cloths; and a piece of canvas to serve as a door for a double camp, together with resin to be used in mending bark canoes. In the absence of resin, the gum obtained from spruce trees will answer the purpose. Care must be taken not to forget the smallest requisite, as the want of an article worth only a few pence will often cause the greatest inconvenience.

The following is the amount of provisions

10

required for a party of four for one month:—The pork is less than would suffice in the event of guns and rods failing to add to the stock.—Pork, thirty pounds; hog's lard, ten pounds; tea, six pounds; brown sugar, twenty pounds; flour, one hundred and forty pounds; tobacco, five pounds; baking powder, four boxes; saleratus, quarter of a pound; half a square of preserved and pressed vegetables; a few pints of beans and split peas; pepper, quarter of a pound; fine salt, one pound; coarse ditto, three pounds—when salmon fishing a greater quantity will be required for curing purposes.

As regards liquor I never take more than a small quantity of rum or whiskey for special occasions. It must always be borne in mind that when hunting in the fall, long portages often have to be made, and everything transported on one's back, every pound in weight tells, and liquor in any quantity is not worth the trouble of "lugging." I always fill up any extra weight with ammunition or food, and at all times reduce my paraphernalia as much as possible, never taking things that I can possibly do without. I am speaking now of a regular hunting trip, miles back from the settlements, where the rivers are the only roads, and where they do not serve, lugging is the order of the day.

Of cooking utensils the same party will require, two frying pans; one small tin despatch oven ; six tin dippers—pannikins—made with curved handles; eight tin dishes, one inch deep; three tin kettles, of the same shape as a milk pail—All these dippers, dishes, and kettles, should be made to fit one inside the other; the largest kettle should hold about two gallons. One large dish for kneading bread; two small boxes for salt and pepper; one larger for sugar. The big kettle is generally used for water, the second size for soup, and the smallest for tea. Matches should be packed in tin boxes, and stowed in different bundles, so that if one lot is destroyed by fire or water, there will still be some left. In addition will be required, three light hunting axes, and one of medium size; one small hatchet, to be kept for butchering purposes, which very soon renders any axe useless for chopping; a couple of common butcher's knives, a good hunting knife—I always used those made by Thornhill, Bond-street—and a few forks and spoons.

If possible, all clothes and provisions should be packed in waterproof bags; those served out to the sappers and gunners are just the thing. Provisions should also be put in separate cotton bags, of which it is well to take a spare supply; these will be useful in case a short cruise is made from the main camp, to reconnoitre, &c. Water-proof stuff to cover everything when travelling in wet weather by canoe, or in winter when hauling, to keep off the snow, is almost indispensable.

The best weapons are a twelve bore breech loading gun, and an express rifle. My guns and rifles were built by Richardson, of Cork, and very good and serviceable weapons they proved, never getting out of order, and only requiring to be held straight. Besides bullets take small shot for birds, and double B for beaver or wild geese. Guns should be always seen to before turning in at night—I make this an invariable rule. Seal skin gun covers, lined with flannel, are the best; all ordinary water-proof covers sweat, and rust the barrel, more than anything else. If out shooting on a wet day, or in snow, tie a strip of flannel, or a long stocking round

your locks; and in case you fall down in the
snow—which is highly probable—always see that
your muzzles are clear.

In winter time, the following extra kit will be
required:—A large camp axe for splitting wood;
a fur hat; two jerseys; several extra pairs of
long stockings and socks; a pair of thick
drawers; a warm waistcoat and shooting jacket
lined with flannel; a pair of mitts; two pairs of
green cow hide mocassins, cut low for snow-
shoeing, and a pair of very long and large stockings, to pull up at night over your trousers. A
white flannel smock over your shooting jacket,
is good for stalking in snow.

Lastly, take care that your snow shoes are good
ones; if they are bad, it will entail endless fatigue
and trouble, as badly made snow shoes, when wet,
" sag,"—become slack. This is very tiring. The
best way to ensure a good pair is to go to an
Indian camp and order them to be made of cariboo hide, promising the man an extra dollar if
he turns out a really good pair. Calf skin is
the best substitute, provided cariboo cannot be
procured. Shoes sold in shops are not to be
depended on, as they are generally scamped

articles, put together without care, merely for sale. The straps of the snow shoe should be made of moose hide or eel skins.

Moose hide mocassins are generally sold in shops; they are well enough in very dry snow, but sag in wet; and I discarded them long ago for the green cow hide, already mentioned, and always used by the natives. Mocassins should be greased at night. Snow shoes, after being worn, ought to be dried at a distance from the fire, and care must be taken not to burn them. A friend of mine did so on one occasion, and discovered in the morning that the strings were ruined, and broke like pack thread. Some strings of cariboo hide, for mending snow shoes, should be put into your "pitsnargan." Take plenty of rope, or thongs of hide, to bind the loads on to the toboggins.

Cooking in camp is a very simple operation. Good bread is the first great requisite, and is prepared in the following way:—Two tea spoons full of baking powder are mixed with a pound of dry flour, and a small pinch of saleratus is dissolved in half a pint of water. The dough must be kneaded stiff, and the cakes made

thin ; they bake best in the tin despatch oven.
Grease in the shape of hog's lard, or melted pork
fat, venison tallow, or even bears' grease, mixed
with the flour, adds very much to the quality
and lightness of the bread.   In the absence of a
despatch oven, put the dough in a frying-pan,
placed at an angle to the fire, or in the ashes, if
your fire has been going a day or two, and there
is a sufficient quantity of them.   Good bread is
also baked without either ashes or utensil of any
kind, in the following manner:—Cut a stick, an
inch in diameter, and two feet long, peel off the
bark and wrap round it spirally a thin strip of
dough; place the stick in the ground at an angle
to the fire, and when the bread is cooked, the
stick will draw out.   This kind of bread is called
in Indian, a "mulquagan," and very sweet and
good it is.

Meat and fish are cooked on sticks placed in
front of the fire, a spatch-cock grouse is excellent
done in this manner. If your cooking pots get
greasy and require cleaning, scrape among the
ashes of an old fire, and you will find lumps of
stuff that appear merely caked ashes, but in
reality are pure potash. Boil some of this in

your kettles, and they will become bright and
clean.

In the way of tents, a light "lean-to" or "half
tent" — of cotton or canvas is preferable to a
double tent, as in the latter the fire cannot be
made in front. A lean-to is much lighter to
carry, and in case you stay long in one place, a
double camp can generally be built. A tent of
any kind is useless in winter, as it is no protection
against cold, and after wet, freezes as hard as a
board. In camping at night select a dry and
sheltered place; if in winter the snow must be
cleared away.

To pitch a lean-to proceed in the following
way:—Cut two poles ten feet high, with crotches
at the tops, and place them upright in the ground,
the width of the tent apart. A pole is then
placed across, resting in the crotches of the
upright poles, which are further secured by being
propped at each end by a forked pole. To the
cross pole is then attached your lean-to, which
is pegged down behind.

To form a bed, a quantity of small boughs
from the fir or hemlock are collected and placed
carefully in rows on the ground, back upwards,

each row overlapping the other like the slates of a house, the stick ends pointing all in the same direction and covered by the soft ends. A pole is then placed at the bottom of the boughs, and secured by pegs. This serves to rest the feet against, and adds immensely to the comfort of the camp, besides preventing your socks being scorched by the heat of the fire when you are asleep. A fireplace is built in front, the back logs of maple or birch, and the dogs of green fir or stones; the fire is kindled with birch bark, which being full of resin, burns in any weather. If there is none to be had, which is not often the case, very dry rotten wood, broken almost into powder, will answer the purpose. A stick serves for a poker, called in Indian "marktaha-gan," the back log "tuan," and the dogs "gym-sihagans." The "chiploquorgan"—already described in the preface—is then stuck in the ground.

For fuel, cut hard wood; yellow birch and rock maple are the best kinds. Hard wood will burn green if well kindled with dry wood, of which a supply must be procured from dead spruce, pine, or other soft wood trees. There is sure to be plenty at hand. Green soft wood will not burn at all. If you have no tent you can either merely put up a blanket or a screen of brush. A party of three or four, each doing his separate share of work, will knock up a temporary camp in a very short time.

Provided you desire a more permanent and water-tight habitation, build a double camp in the following manner:—Mark out on the ground a rectangular figure, ten feet by two; select four poles of equal length with crotches at the tops, and stick them perpendicularly into the ground at the angles of the figure. Place two poles parallel to each other, and lengthwise to the figure, their ends resting in the crotches of the uprights, and lashed firm.   Lay on the ground without the two longer sides of the rectangle, and at a distance of four feet, two logs one above the other, each pair of logs to be parallel to the poles resting in the crotches, and secured in their places on either side by pegs driven into the ground. These logs serve as a walling to the camp. Cut a number of poles and place them slanting over the walling, their lower ends stuck in the ground, the upper ends resting on the poles in the crotches; the two outside slanting poles should be lashed at the top and bottom; they should also be secured by cross sticks, lashed high up. The sides should be filled up with poles stuck in the ground, and leaning against the outside slanters at a slight angle. The space between the upright crotches is left open on one side for the entrance. The frame of the camp is now complete.

The covering varies according to the locality, and time of year. The best roof is spruce bark, which in summer peels off easily in large sheets ; next comes birch bark, which is of two kinds— winter, that peels in spring and autumn, and summer, from June to August. In winter time no bark will peel, and splints must be used. These are split from pine or cedar. In the absence of these trees, spruce, and even fir, will answer the purpose. The cedar is by no means a general tree in the forest, it only grows in swampy places, and is not found at all in Nova Scotia. With respect to lashings—if you have not any rope—in summer, the inner bark of the cedar, or the roots of the spruce, are used. In winter, when these cannot be procured, withes, of wild cherry, birch, and some kinds of shrubs, warmed at the fire and then twisted, form a sub-stitute. The roof of bark or splints is kept in its place by heavy poles, placed leaning against it. The top of the camp is left open in the centre. At the sides it is covered with brush or bark. In winter, snow is piled up outside to keep out the wind. The fire place is built in the centre, and as the occupants of the camp lie either side, no tuan is required.

In a double camp the chiploquorgan is differ-ent to that used in a single one ; it is arranged in the following way :—A stick is cut of birch or cherry, with a crook in the bottom, the twigs being left at the top, these are twisted so as to form a loop, by which the stick is suspended over the fire from a cross pole at the top of the camp. The kettles are then hung on the crook. A camp of this description will take two smart Indians a couple of days to build, unless the materials, such as bark or splints, are very near at hand. In such a dwelling you may, provided you have a good fire, defy any weather. It does not do to trust entirely to Indians to cut enough wood to last a cold night, or you may find your fuel "give out" before morning. If this happens, turn them at once to cut wood by torchlight, moon-light, or even in the dark.

A half camp is covered only on one side, the other being left open, and the fire placed in front. As a rule I should recommend a half-tent for use in summer, or the fall, when moving about ; but if a halt in one place for any length of time is contemplated, set to work at once and build a double camp. The trouble is slight, and you will probably be driven by the weather to do so before long. In winter, a half-camp is a miserably cold affair to live in for any time, and you require an enormous amount of fuel to keep from freezing on a severe night, as I have more than once practically discovered.

Deer skins are cured by stretching on a frame, composed of two poles fixed in the ground, and two others lashed to them at right angles. Slits are cut in the edge of the hide, about six inches apart, and it is then laced tightly to the frame with string or spruce roots. In fine weather, it will dry in a few days; but in case the weather is wet, put up your frames sufficiently near a fire to warm the inside of the hide.

Skins dried gradually by the fire, keep better, and the hair is firmer than those dried in the sun. In winter time, the frost will dry them, provided they do not get frozen before they are stretched, in which case they will have to be thawed before putting on the frames. Care should be taken to scrape off all the fat from the hides, for where fat is left, if the weather is warm, the flies are sure to strike the hair, which soon comes out. No salt or any preserving mixture is required.

The proper mode to prepare and preserve the heads of large animals for stuffing, is the following:—Cut off the head, leaving a good long neck; slit up the back of the neck to within a few inches of the horns; make two branch cuts up to, and close round the root of each antler. The skin is then turned back and stripped altogether off the head. Remove the flesh from the skull and jaw bone; if there is a black ant's nest near, bury them in it. Cut all the sinews and tendons of the lip by slashing with a knife inside. This prevents the lip contracting when dry. Finally, paint the skin inside all over, with the following mixture dissolved in spirits until about the thickness of cream:—Arsenic, one pound; curd soap, one pound; salts of tartar, quarter pound; lime, quarter pound; camphor, quarter pound. Half a dozen applications of this mixture, laid on with a brush, will cure a head perfectly; it will also keep soft, and the hair will never become loose, which is invariably the case if salt is used.   In fact, salt is ruination to any skin, of which the hair or fur is to be kept on, and skins so preserved will not last any time, the hair always coming out.   This will also be the result in the event of an animal being killed when perspiring from being chased, either on land or in the water, especially the latter.

Steel traps are undoubtedly the surest and best method of capturing fur bearing animals; but their exclusive use is precluded both by the expense and the enormous additional weight a large quantity of them would entail.   It is better therefore to take a couple of dozen only, and use them chiefly for otter and beaver.   In winter beavers cannot be killed by any other means. Make the remainder of your traps of wood— commonly called dead-falls—which have this advantage—that, whereas, steel traps have to be carried, all the materials for a dead-fall are everywhere at hand in the woods.

The only places where good steel traps are
manufactured is Western Canada and the United
States.   At Bangor, in the State of Maine,
excellent traps are made at a very reasonable
price.   The great desideratum is lightness, combined with strength and proper shape.   The
traps made in England are heavy and clumsy,
and constructed on an entirely wrong principle.
The pans, which should not be bigger than a
crown piece, are three inches square, and the
jaws are of the wrong shape and not high enough.
In fact, English traps are not worth their carriage
into the woods.

A few years ago I sent an American steel
trap of the newest and lightest kind to a maker
at Wolverhampton as a pattern, but this man
charged more to copy it than the trap originally
cost in the States, for the reason that it was so
unlike his own wretched articles, that he would
have had to make new moulds for the castings.
A Yankee maker would not have failed to have
seen the improvement and executed the order,
glad to pick up a wrinkle; not so the obtuse,
obstinate Britisher, who refused to profit by it,
fearing the first outlay, though the traps could

be made for far less in England than in the United States.

Dead-falls are constructed somewhat after the manner of the figure 4. In the fall they are built on the ground; in winter, on the top of a stump, or in a hollow or rotten tree, high enough up to prevent their being snowed up. The traps are placed about a hundred yards apart in a straight line, the trees being blazed at short intervals to enable the line to be easily followed. A good Indian will build from twelve to fifteen traps in a day.

Traps should be overhauled about every five days to take out animals and renew baits eaten by mice or squirrels. In the event of rain, followed by immediate frost, all dead-falls will be frozen up and must be re-set. The bait most generally used is deer meat; fish is good, especially for mink. The flesh of musk rats, squirrels and grouse is also used. The baits should be scented to attract the animals, either with a few drops of oil obtained from decomposed eels or trout, by hanging them in a bottle in the sun, or by a mixture of musquash musk, beaver castors and Indian tobacco root dissolved in spirit. It is

11

a good plan to trail a piece of meat along the line, as animals will often follow the scent and consequently come across the traps.

Steel traps when set for land fur should be placed at the entrance of an enclosure of boughs or sticks, and so situated that the animal must step on the trap to get at the bait, which should be tied to the end of a stick placed firmly into the ground at the furthest end of the enclosure. The trap when set should be carefully concealed by leaves or fine powdered rotten wood. Never place a bait on the pan of a trap; English traps are always made with holes in the pan for string to tie on the bait, so as to attract the animal to the centre of action, as though it was expected to catch him by the head. The truth is that animals are rarely taken by the head, but nearly always by a leg. When an animal begins to pull at a bait tied on the pan, he would not even be likely to spring the trap, for he lifts in the wrong direction, and if he does spring it, he is very unlikely to be caught. Moreover, bait on the pan calls the attention of the wary animal to the trap, whereas he ought to be wholly diverted from it, and all signs of it obliterated.

The great object is to place the trap so that the animal on seizing the bait will place his foot upon the pan.

The season for trapping is from the 1st of November to the middle of April for land fur; water fur, such as otters, beavers, and musk rats is good from the 1st of October to the end of April. The state of a skin is detected by looking at the inside, which, when the fur is in prime order, is white, at other times it is more or less of a darker shade.

The chain of a steel trap set on land should not be fastened to a stake driven into the ground, or the animal in his struggles to free himself may break the hold and get out, perhaps leaving his foot or toe in the trap. A long green pole should be cut, with the top branches left on, the ring at the end of the chain being slid over the butt, which must then be wedged to prevent its slipping off, or it may be secured by a bit of cord. This plan allows the animal play, and effectually prevents his escape, as the pole is sure to get caught in the bushes before he has dragged it many yards.

There is another plan of securing a steel trap

on land by what is called a spring pole; this contrivance prevents animals gnawing off their feet, and also provides against their being devoured by other beasts before the trapper reaches them. It is prepared in the undermentioned method. If a small hard wood tree can be found growing near where your trap is set, trim it and use it as a spring as it stands; if not, cut a pole of sufficient size and drive it firmly into the ground, bending down the top to which is fastened the chain ring; the top is then secured in its bent position by a notch in a tree or stake. When the animal is caught, his struggles release the pole which flies up and suspends him in the air, out of the reach of prowlers, and unable to escape by self-amputation or other violence.

CHAPTER XI.

Fur bearing animals of Canada—Beavers— Interesting particulars
regarding them—Different modes of hunting beaver—How to trap
beavers through the ice—Musk rats—The American otter—
Description of the mink—Habits and value of the sable—The
fisher, and how to catch it—Sagacity of the animal—Descriptions of the lynx, racoon, skunk, wood chuck, American fox and
squirrel—Particulars concerning their habits—" The Indian
devil"—How to dry skins of fur—Wild fruits and flowers.

THE following are the fur bearing animals of
North America, the most curious of which is the
beaver (*castor fiber*). So much has already
been written respecting the habits of this animal,
that it appears superfluous for me to add to it.
But as many of the more ancient descriptions
teem with exaggerations and fallacies, I shall
briefly touch upon the subject, as perhaps some
of my readers may not have read the more
modern and accurate writings.

The beaver formerly—when his fur was made

into hats—was the most valuable animal to the trapper, and was hunted to such an extent that he is now extinct in many parts of North America; but the wild meadows that are met with all over the country bear witness to his labours, even after all traces of his dams have disappeared. These meadows have been formed by the damming of a small brook, which over-flowing more or less, has killed the trees which rotted and fell. The dam having been destroyed by man, or deserted by the beavers, the waters resume their original course, and the hitherto flooded land becomes a meadow. Grass springs up, and the former site of the pond is not covered over with a fresh growth of trees, as would be the case if the woods were cleared by fire or the axe.

The beaver has a thick heavy body, two feet and a half long when full grown, and weighing about sixty pounds. The tail is a notable part of the animal, and measures from ten to twelve inches in length, and from three to four in circumference; it is oval in shape, but flattened on the upper and under sides and covered with a species of hairy scales, which are set upon a thick dusky skin. The tail answers as a kind of prop to enable the animal to raise itself up when at work; it also serves as a rudder and oar when swimming, being turned under the body with great rapidity and power like the operation of sculling a boat. If suddenly frightened while swimming, he strikes the water violently with his tail, producing a loud whack as a signal of danger to others of his tribe, and disappears altogether beneath the surface.

Beavers are not gregarious in summer, but become so on the approach of autumn when they build or repair their houses and dams. The houses are built at a height of four or five feet out of the water with their entrances at the bottom under water; they have the appearance of a heap of mud and sticks, and are about the size of two hay cocks made into one. The houses are not plastered down smooth on the outside like an ant hill, as has been stated. On the contrary the sticks and mud are thrown together any how, and totally devoid of order. A single house generally contains from four to ten animals, all of the same family and of different generations. Beavers that inhabit large lakes or deep sluggish rivers do not build dams, as they have plenty of water, but make their houses along the banks. Those that live in small streams where the water is shallow build a dam, so as to raise the water and form a pond of sufficient depth to prevent their winter stores of provisions, which are collected in the immediate vicinity of the house, from freezing up.

The beaver cuts down trees of all sizes from ten inches thick to the smallest brushwood. I have seen a tree of a foot in diameter cut by a beaver. Their front teeth, with which they cut, are shaped like a rabbit's, and of immense strength; they drag a large bit of wood along by their teeth, laying one paw over it; mud, small sticks, and stones are carried between the fore-paws and the chin. It is a popular error to suppose that these animals use their tails as trowels to plaster down the mud used in the construction of their dams and houses. There is no outward finish in the dams any more than in their houses. The height is uniform, and the water drips evenly from one end to the other. The dams are sometimes six or seven feet high and thirty to forty yards in length. On the approach of the fall, after new dams are built or old ones repaired, they lay in their winter stock of provisions, consisting of the bark of the willow, poplar, alder, white and yellow birch, and other hard wood trees. They fell these trees, and then cut them into short lengths and sink them in the water near their houses. In winter when the ponds are frozen over, they drag these sunken sticks into their dwellings as they require food, eat off the bark quite clean, and throw them outside again.

The breeding season of the beaver commences in May, and they have from two to four at a birth. When a habitation, from the increase of the family, becomes too small, a new colony is started. They generally go up stream to build a new dam. In some brooks I have seen dams, so numerous, that the water from one set back to the next above. There are no separate cells or apartments in a beaver's house, it is merely a large hollow place. Besides the bark of the above mentioned trees, the beaver feeds on the roots of various aquatic plants, of the water lily species.

Solitary beavers are sometimes met with, liv-

ing in holes in banks; these, the Indians say,
have been turned out of their houses for idleness.
But I think it is more probable that they are the
remains of a family, the rest of whom have been
killed by the trapper. Beavers can be caught
in the fall by dead-falls, set in their hauling
roads, of which there are always several leading
from a pond, and which they use when dragging
sticks, either for their houses, dams, or for food.
But steel traps are almost indispensable for a
campaign against these animals.

There are several ways of killing beaver without traps, of which shooting affords the best
sport. When the animals swim about their
ponds of an evening, the hunter hides himself
close to the house, and kills them as they make
their appearance. If one is wounded, no more
will come out, as has already been practically
shown in these pages. I have several times
shot beaver in this way. Double B. shot should
be used for this purpose. Another plan is to
break the dams and pull down the houses; this
can only be done when the dams are situated in
small brooks, as it would be impossible to drain
a large lake. As soon as the water has run off,

you knock the beavers on the head, or spear them. A dog is useful on such an occasion, as they will often hide under the banks, where a good dog will ferret them out. Any beavers left in a dam, after it has been broken, leave the place altogether that night, and a trap set at the outlet and the inlet of the dam, is sure to be successful.

It is not a good plan to break dams, when trapping any time in a neighbourhood, as by slower means, you may catch the whole family, add to which, a dam, if not damaged, is likely to have a fresh colony the next year. Other methods are, to set steel traps under water, in the runs leading to their houses, and in small breaches made in the dam for that purpose, as the animals will know from the water falling, that there is a leak, and repairing the same at night will probably be caught at work. Steel traps are also effectively set in their roads. To attract the animals, a stick should be placed above the trap, rubbed with a beaver's castor, a powerful smelling bag taken from the inside of the animal.

Care should be taken not to make much

noise, or otherwise disturb the animals, where you have your traps, or the whole family may clear out and quit the place. If you have plenty of time, it is better not to set any traps close to the house, but to put them in suitable places at some distance, in order that the beaver when caught may be alone, and, therefore, unable to create a general alarm. The traps should be secured by the chain ring to a pole, as already described; and if the trap is placed under water, which is generally the case, attach a stone to it, in order that on a captured animal getting into deep water, the weight may sink and drown him. Beaver traps should be visited every two or three days, or you will probably only catch toes and feet, the animals having escaped by self amputation.

In winter, when the ponds are frozen, there is but one way of trapping beaver, and that is the following:—At that time of the year, on the discovery of a house, the first fact to be ascertained is, whether it be inhabited. Every thing is covered with several feet of snow; there are no fresh cuttings or well used roads to indicate the presence of the animals. The means of finding out this most necessary fact is simple and easy, but I doubt whether it would occur to one man out of a thousand. It is ascertained by scraping away the snow from the top of the house, and if it be inhabited the snow will be more or less melted close to the earth, in the form of a cone, caused by the heat of the animals inside, rising up and thawing it. This is an infallible test, and was first shown me by Joe Bear, and subsequently I have often seen this melting of the snow at the top of the house—called by Indians, " The smoke hole." The presence of the beavers having been discovered in the above-mentioned manner, the next thing is to find out the whereabouts of the run, leading to the entrance. This is done by trying with your axe, where the ice is thinnest, here, will be the run, as the constant disturbing of the water by the beavers, in their ingress and egress, tends to make the ice weakest in that spot. You will also see plenty of peeled sticks in the immediate vicinity of the run; the bark having been eaten off, the sticks are drawn out of the house and cast on one side. Having thus found the run, a hole is cut in the ice, eighteen inches square, directly over it, and

a yard or so from the entrance to the house.
Two stakes of yellow birch or poplar, about two
inches in diameter, are then driven firmly into
the earth, through the hole already cut in the
ice, opposite one another, and the width of the
hole apart. Inside these stakes, touching and
parallel to them, are placed two sticks of the
same wood, about the thickness of a man's finger.

Having set your trap, let it down carefully
with a hooked stick, and place it on the bottom
between the upright stakes, a few inches nearer
one than the other, so that the beaver may not
gnaw either stake, and escape being caught by
having the trap between his legs, which might
happen if the trap was in the centre; but as it
is fixed he is likely to be caught by the fore leg,
in the event of his cutting the stick nearest
the trap, by the hind leg in the reverse case.
The chain ring must be firmly wedged on to a
soft wood pole of fir or spruce, and driven into
the ground about a yard from the trap, a nick
being cut in the ice for that purpose. A soft
wood pole is used for the reason that beavers do
not feed on soft wood. If it was hard wood they
might attack the chain stake, instead of the bait

sticks, to which they are attracted by their being newly cut.

If when putting down the trap, the water gets muddy from the animals coming out, on hearing a disturbance near their dwellings, a thin sheet of white birch bark is fastened at the bottom of the trap; this will act as a reflector, and enable the person setting the trap, to see that it is properly placed.

All the beavers we captured when at the Little South West, Mirimichi Lake, were taken under the ice in this manner. It was rather exciting, when on looking down at your trap, you saw a big beaver fast at the bottom.

In the spring of the year, when the ice begins to thaw, the water round a beaver house is generally open before other parts of the lake or pond. The beavers swim about in the open place, so by waiting behind a bush placed on the ice, you can shoot them as they come out.

The musk rat, or "musquash" (*fiber zibethicus*) inhabits all parts of North America, and is, like the beaver, an animal of amphibious habits, and also somewhat resembles it in shape. His length is from thirteen to fifteen inches; the tail about nine inches long, is edged like a file and covered with scales and thin short hair. The hind feet are webbed. Musk rats generally feed at night, their principal food is grass and roots. They chiefly inhabit muddy lakes and sluggish streams, bordered with reeds and flags. They live for the most part in holes in the banks. In lakes they sometimes build houses with sticks and mud, the entrance being under water. In winter also they have little houses, built in the shallow parts of lakes, for the purpose of feeding in. These houses look like so many heaps of grass, about the size of a man's hat. On taking off the top, a small dry space is disclosed, just big enough for a rat to sit in and eat the food he has procured in the vicinity, under the water. A small steel trap set in these dining rooms, is sure to catch him. They are also caught by traps set under water in their runs. But the most destructive method is to dig them out of their holes in autumn. Hundreds are killed in this way in the St. John river, which, from its many lakes and dead waters, abounds with these animals. They are also caught in floating box-traps, baited with a parsnip or carrot.

When the spring freshets take place, the rats are flooded out of their holes, by the rising waters, and hide among reeds or bushes along the banks. This is also the commencement of the breeding season of these most prolific animals. They are at this time of year, called and shot. You place yourself in the bow of a canoe, with an Indian behind, who paddles carefully along, and calls with his mouth, somewhat in the manner an English keeper will call a stoat. When at Fredericton I had many a days' amusement, calling, and shooting musk rats, and sometimes killed dozens in a day. Their skins are worth from ten pence to a shilling each.

The American otter, (*lutra Canadensis,*) found in all parts of North America, does not differ from the European species, except that the fur is darker and thicker. It is rambling in its habits, and feeds entirely on fish. In winter their tracks may be seen in the snow, at some distance from any water, as they will travel miles from one lake or stream to the nearest point of another. These animals have a singular practice of sliding down wet and muddy banks, or slopes, apparently for sport. It requires time

12

and patience to take them, as although you may
see fresh tracks and set your trap, it may be ten
or twelve days before the animals re-visit the
spot in their circuitous wanderings.

Otters may be taken in dead-falls set in their
roads leading to the water near a slide, or
especially in a trap set at the top of an old
beaver dam, a breach being made in it, and
sticks being so placed as to guide him into the
trap,—a steel trap being, of course, by far the
most certain method.   In the fall, the trap is set
a few inches under water, near a slide, so as to
catch the otter as he lands; he does not come
ashore directly on to the slide—which is that part
of the bank of the stream or lake which inclines
at a steep angle into the water—so that the animal may plunge from the slide into deep water
without obstruction.   On landing, he chooses a
place where the water is shallow, and where he
can easily walk up the bank; there the trap
should be set a few inches under water, and a
little on one side of the path of the animal, for
the legs of the otter stand out on the sides of his
body, and are so far apart that he is likely to put
down his feet on each side of the trap, and not

in it, if it is set in the middle of his track. The
trap, if possible, should be placed at the point
where the animal's feet strike the bottom on
approaching the shore. Another plan is to set
the trap at the top of the slide where the animal
starts for his descent, he will then be probably
on his legs, whereas, in the middle of the slide,
he would be rolling, and apt to spring the trap
with his breast or belly, and escape being seized
by the jaws. The trap should be placed on the
side of the path, as above described, in a hole
made in the earth for that purpose, deep enough
to bring the jaws nearly level with the ground ;
the whole should then be covered with leaves, or
fine rotten wood, placed to look as natural as
possible. A few sticks, or bits of brush, should
be thrown down in a careless way, to guide the
animal to the trap. The chain-ring of the trap,
wherever it is placed, should be fastened to a
young tree, with branches left on, as before described.

When the ice sets in, and the slides can no
longer be used, steel traps must be set at spring
holes, and at the entrance or outlet of a lake,
where the water does not freeze. Here the

otter will pass, as the only way of getting under the ice for the purpose of fishing. The trap should be placed a few inches under water, so as to take him either as he leaves the water or enters it. Traps can also be set in open spots, in shallow, quick-running brooks; for otters, traversing a stream in the winter, come out at an opening in the ice, walk along the top, and take the water at the next open place they come to: they also always come out of the water to dung. If the water is too deep at the entrance or outlet of a lake for the trap to be set on the bottom, make a platform of brush, so situated that the animal will be likely to climb over it, and on this place your trap, which should be under water. The skin of an otter, in good order, is worth from seven to eight dollars.

The mink *(mustela vison)*, inhabits most parts of Canada ; it resembles in shape the ferret, and is of a dark-brown color, with short legs, long body and neck, and a bushy tail. Though not amphibious, they frequent the banks of streams, feeding chiefly on fish, but will devour meat of any kind. Their breeding season commences in May, and the females have from four to eight at a litter. The skins of these animals are worth from four to five dollars each, and the fur is in good order from October to the middle of April. They are taken in dead-falls and steel traps, but are at all times difficult to catch, and in very cold weather will hardly bite at all. I have seen where they had passed close to a trap, of which they seemed to have taken no notice. The best bait for these animals is fish scented with fish oil, obtained in the manner before referred to.

The marten, commonly known as the sable, (*mustela zebellina*), is about the same size as the mink, and differs little from it in form, save that its feet are larger, and hairy to the toes ; its tail is also somewhat larger. It makes a straggling track in the snow, like that of an English hare ; whereas, the mink moves by a series of jumps, the feet being brought close together at each spring. The fur of the marten is longer than that of the mink, and varies in color from a light buff to a very dark brown. The price of the skin varies in America from three to five dollars, according to the color ; the darker the shade the more valuable, and the further north he is found the darker the fur. The darkest and most valuable sables come from Russia and northern China. The favourite haunts of the sable are thick forests, especially of hard wood growth ; they are arboreal in their habitat, and generally live in hollow stumps, or in trees.   Their food consists of rabbits, mice, squirrels, and other small animals.   They are capital climbers, and chase squirrels.   They breed in April, and have four or five young at a time.

Sable are taken in dead-falls and steel traps, the same as set for mink.   " A sable line," as it is called, is generally set across hard wood ridges, or mixed growth.   Deer meat is the most general bait ; but any flesh will answer the purpose, and fish will do.   It is a capital plan to set a couple of traps alongside where you have killed a deer ; the smell of blood is sure to attract any carniverous animals that are in the immediate neighbourhood.   At the same time you must carefully bury in the snow, or cover with earth, all bits of meat or entrails left on the spot.

The fisher, (*mustela penante*,)—sometimes miscalled the pekin—resembles the marten in its habits, though much larger than that animal; its general shape is somewhat similar, though the head is more pointed, the ears more rounded, the neck, legs, and feet stouter, and the claws much stronger. An averaged sized fisher will measure two feet from the nose to the tail, which is large and bushy. The fur is dark grey, tipped with black, and a skin is worth from seven to eight dollars.

The fisher feeds like the sable, and does not live principally on fish, as its name would imply, but will take any bait of either fish or flesh. He requires a much stronger trap than the mink or marten, and is also far more cunning. The usual plan in building a line, is to make every tenth trap purposely strong, and heavily weighted for this animal; not only will the dead-fall of an ordinary sable trap be too light to kill him, but he will follow a line and tear down the traps from the top or behind, and so get at the bait, without any chance of being caught. A fisher trap must be built up and so secured with heavy logs that he cannot get at the bait without springing the dead-fall. A strong steel trap is the best method of taking him, set in the manner already mentioned. His track is of the same kind as the marten, but larger. The fisher is,

in comparison with the mink and marten, a very
scarce animal.

The Canadian lynx *(felis Canadensis)*—called
by the settlers the loupcervier—is common in
all parts of Canada. In size it is between that
of a fox and a wolf; its length about three feet,
the tail only an inch long is furred and tipped
with black; the ears are small and pointed, the
feet large, and the colour of the skin a light grey.
This animal frequents chiefly low swampy land
and thick growth of spruce, where the American
hare—the favourite food of the lynx—chiefly
resorts. He never attacks a deer, but feeds on
all small animals that come within his reach.
He is easily caught in dead-falls or steel traps;
the latter placed at the entrance of a house built
for the purpose, and baited with a hare or piece
of meat. The skin is worth two and a half
dollars, and is used for making sleigh robes.

The above-mentioned animals are those chiefly
sought by the trappers, and to take them special
means are adopted. In addition there are several
other species of little or no value.

The racoon *(procyon lotor)* is common in
North America; its body is about two feet long

and thick and stout; the colour is greyish white, streaked with darker shades. This animal is nocturnal and omniverous in its habits, and hibernates like the bear. It feeds on nuts, corn, small animals, and birds; is a good climber, and lives in trees. The skin does not fetch above a dollar.

The skunk (*mustela Americana*) is often met with, the body eighteen inches long; in colour white, with a black streak down the middle. This animal is not sought after; its smell is abominable, and the fur almost worthless.

The woodchuck or ground hog (*arctomys monax*) or Maryland marmot, is a small animal of the size of a hedgehog. It lives in holes, and the skin is sometimes used by Indians for small bags to hold tobacco.

The American fox (*canis fulvus*) is generally of rather a lighter colour than the European species. Of these animals the black and silver grey have the most valuable fur that the country produces, and are exceedingly rare, especially the black fox. A man might spend his lifetime trapping and not take one. These valuable varieties do not belong to a separate breed, but are merely a freak of nature and accidental. They are more numerous in the Island of Anticosti than any parts of North America. This island, I may mention, contains neither beaver nor deer of any kind. A silver grey fox is worth fifty dollars; a black fox, one hundred and fifty dollars.

There are several kinds of squirrels in Canada, the grey squirrel (*sciurus leucotis*), the red, (*a rufa*) or red marmot, the ground, (*a tridecion lineata*) or Wood's marmot. The grey species is not found in the Maritime provinces, both the others are common, of which the ground squirrel is a hibernating animal.

There are several kinds of snakes in the Maritime provinces of Canada, but all of a harmless nature. The rattle-snake only frequents the more western parts of Canada, and is found in great numbers in the prairies of the United States.

The wolverine (*gulo wolverine*), often called the "Indian Devil," is very rarely met with in the Maritime provinces of Canada, but inhabits the more northern regions, formerly occupied by the Hudson Bay Company. In general appearance it resembles a bear, with a head something like a fisher. It is powerfully built, possesses great strength, and climbs with much agility. The prevailing colour is dark brown, the legs and feet are black, the fur is long and rather soft. These beasts follow lines of traps, tearing them down and taking out the baits and animals that may be caught. Indians have a sort of superstitious dread of these animals. I once heard at night on the Mirimichi waters a most hideous howling, and was told by Sebattis it was an Indian Devil.

Having succeeded in catching your fur, the next consideration is to take care that your skins are not damaged but are properly stretched and dried. To insure this the animal should be skinned as soon as possible after it is caught, except in frosty weather, or the skin will become tainted, in which case it is spoilt beyond redemption. Scrape off all the superfluous flesh and fat, and be careful not to cut the fibre of the hide. After the skin is stretched, the mode of doing which I shall presently describe, let it dry in the shade, and in the event of rain bring it into your camp, and dry it by the warmth of the fire, but very gradually. Do not use salt or preparation of any kind, but simply stretch and dry the skins as they are taken from the animals. This does not of course apply to the curing of heads for stuffing, which should be treated in the manner already mentioned.

In drying skins it is needful that they should be stretched tight like a drum head. There are three kinds of stretchers used in curing fur-bearing animals—the bow stretcher, the board stretcher and the hoop stretcher. The bow stretcher is a common and clumsy way of treating a skin, and is generally confined to the musk rat or other fur of small value. It is merely a pliant stick bent in the form of an oxbow, and then shoved into the skin, the fur being inside, which is taken off the animal like a rabbit by cutting at the vent, and then drawing the skin back over the body up to the nose. A shingle rounded off at the end is often used instead of the oxbow.

The board stretcher, a much neater and more elaborate contrivance, is used for the more valuable furs, such as marten, mink, fisher and otters. The following is the mode in which it is manufactured:—Prepare a splint of cedar, spruce, or other soft wood, two feet three inches

long, three inches and a-half wide at one end,
two inches and a-half at the other, and a quarter
of an inch thick; fine it down with a crooked
knife from the centre to the sides, almost to
an edge, round and shave the small end about
an inch up on the sides.   Divide this splint
through the centre with a knife or small saw.
Lastly, prepare a wedge of the same length and
thickness, one inch wide at the large end, and
tapering to three-eights at the narrow.   Remove
the skin from the animal, by splitting down the
hind feet to the vent; cut round the vent, and
strip the skin from the tail with the fingers or a
split stick—in the otter the tail requires to be
split.open—pull the skin off by drawing it over
the body up to the nose.   The skin is then drawn
over the two splints—fur inside—the back one
side, the belly the other, to its utmost length,
and the wedge is driven in between the two
halves, and the skin secured from slipping
back by tacks or wooden pegs at the tail.   A
stretcher of the above dimensions is of the size
for mink or sable ; for otter, fisher, or lynx, a
larger would be required.   The hoop-stretcher
is always used for beaver, and is simply a hoop
of hazel, or other pliant wood.

The beaver is skinned by cutting down the belly from the lower front teeth to the vent, but without slitting up the legs ; the hide should then be lashed all round to the hoop with string, or a substitute, and drawn perfectly tight. There is often a good deal of fat on a beaver; so care should be taken to scrape it off, for wherever fat is left the skin will not dry, and the fur will come out. In fine weather, four or five days will suffice to dry skins thoroughly, in which state they will keep for years, if not destroyed by moths.

There is a great absence of wild flowers in North America compared to England, and of the kinds that are found but few have any smell. The most characteristic flower of the country is the may-flower, which has a delicious perfume, and springs up almost before the snow has disappeared. It is a dwarf plant, with the individual flowers somewhat of the shape of those of a lilac, but grooped together like the laurestinus. In the early spring, may-flower picnics are got up, as the plant is by no means general, and only grows in certain localities. Primroses and violets are not indigenous to North America.

On the other hand, wild fruits—such as strawberries, raspberries, blueberries and cranberries—are found in great profusion. Raspberries and strawberries always spring up spontaneously wherever the land has been cleared, especially if by fire. These berries are of excellent flavour, and are sold in the markets at a shilling a bucketful. They are in season as follows :— strawberries, early in July ; raspberries, in August ; blueberries, in September ; cranberries, in October. Of the latter there are four kinds— the rock, the marsh, the high bush and the low bush, of which the rock is the best fruit.

CHAPTER XII.

General description of Canada—The civilized red Indians—Singularity
of dress—The Micmac and Milicite tribes—The Mohawk and
Labrador Indians—Difference in building canoes—Indian superstition—Improvidence of the natives—Peculiarities of their habits
—The Indian and negro contrasted—Canadian settlers—Aspect,
produce, resources, and manufactories of the various provinces.

HAVING described the sporting capabilities of
Canada, a few words upon the inhabitants, and a
slight review of the country at the present time,
may not be without some interest.   The Indians,
as the oldest possessors of the soil, are entitled to
the first place.   These people are fast dying out
from consumption, and other diseases, brought
on a good deal by frequent inter-marriages.   The
civilized Indian of the present day, as a rule,
wear nothing national in the way of attire.   They
dress like other people, with the difference that
their clothes are more ragged and dirty.   They
are very fond of wearing a black coat.   I have

seen an Indian in the remains of what was once a frock coat with velvet collar. At Fredericton there was a sprinkling of officers' worn out shooting jackets to be seen, presents after a trip in the woods, and eagerly sought after; an Indian named Noel Lolah used to wear a coat of the loudest check.

In the Maritime provinces of Canada there are two tribes of Indians, the Micmac and the Milicite. Of these the Micmac is by far the more numerous and powerful; in former days they drove the Milicites out of part of New Brunswick. The Micmacs originally belonged to Nova Scotia, from whence they have spread more or less over the neighbouring provinces, especially in the northern part of New Brunswick. The Micmac Indians of Nova Scotia are the best hunters to be found in the country, but they are not so neat in their work as the Milicites. Their canoes, paddles, &c., are larger and more clumsily manufactured; their squaws' fancy work is made with porcupine quills dyed, and worked in different patterns on boxes, &c., made of birch bark.

The Milicites inhabit parts of New Brunswick and the State of Maine, their headquarters being

13

on the St. John river. There is a great jealousy
between the two tribes; the Milicites hating the
Micmacs, and the Micmacs effecting to despise
the Milicites. At the present time there are but
few Indians of either tribe who are really good
hunters, especially in New Brunswick, where the
Micmacs do less hunting of the two, living chiefly
by making baskets and butter tubs. This is
more or less the trade of all of them, with the
exception of the manufacture of mocassins, snow
shoes, and canoes. Some of these men are
excellent coopers, using only a crooked knife and
an axe, with which they make tubs; these are
beautifully fitted, quite water tight, and hooped
with pieces of ground ash in lieu of iron. Their
baskets are made of white ash, split very thin,
and dyed different colours.

Old Sebattis was one of the few Indians who
thoroughly knew his business as a hunter in all
its branches. He was an excellent hand with
an axe or crooked knife, and built a first-rate
canoe. Nothing ever came amiss to him. In
building a camp his equal was rarely to be met
with, and he was one of the best polers in a
canoe I ever saw.

The fancy articles manufactured by the Milicites are principally bead work, with which they embroider mocassins, belts, &c. The colours are well blended, and some of the patterns beautifully designed.

In the Northern provinces of Canada there are Mohawks and other tribes; also some of the Milicites in the neighbourhood of Quebec. Few, if any of the Indians in these regions understand either the art of moose calling, or that of creeping without snow. From Quebec and Montreal comes the beautiful moose hair work, which is the most handsome and valuable of any of the fancy articles made by the Indians. The Labrador Indians make the most beautifully finished bark canoes of any of the Indian tribes. They are rather smaller than those of the Milicites, which are low, long and narrow, with a straight bow, and capable of being carried on a man's back. A full sized Micmac canoe is much wider and higher, the nose is rounded, and two men are required to portage it.

The ribs, frame and flooring of a birch canoe are of cedar, the cross bars, rock maple; and the bark covering is sewn with spruce roots; the

seams being made water tight by a mixture of resin
and grease laid over them. Good bark is now
getting very scarce, and a canoe costs twelve
dollars. The Milicite paddles are beautifully
shaped, and of the most perfect symmetry. The
Micmac more rounded in the blade, and not so
well finished. The snow shoes of all tribes differ,
the Micmac being round at the toes, the Milicite,
as is the case with their paddles, more pointed.
In Labrador the snow shoes used by the Esqui-
maux are almost circular.

It is curious to observe the same ideas and
differences of shape pervading the whole paraphernalia of a tribe, from the mocassin to the
snow shoe, and from the axe handle to the canoe.

These Indians have their native doctors who
pretend to be able to cure all kinds of diseases;
they are also exceedingly superstitious. At one
time when travelling in the woods and camping
at dusk, I sent the Indian to get some birch bark,
of which there was none very near. He returned
looking quite scared; on my asking him what
was the matter, he replied, " Me no like to camp
here, my father see Devil here once." On being
further questioned, he related that his father,

when hunting some cariboo in a barren close by, saw a man in the dress of the old French settlers walking in snow shoes.   After firing at the deer, his father returned to speak to the man he had seen, and following his tracks they suddenly came to an end! Nor were there any back tracks!   "You laugh," said the Indian, "but my father see Devil sure enough and no mistake." However, camp there we did to the great disgust of the Indian, who hardly slept during the night, being doubtless in terror of seeing the same apparition as appeared to his father.

All Indians are named after saints, Joe, Peter, and Noel being the most common appellations; a Dick or Bob is never heard of; they are also particularly fond of money, but squander it as soon as earned.   A man to whom you have perhaps paid forty dollars after a hunting trip, will come in a week and ask you to lend him a dollar.   "Where is all the money I gave you, Peter?"   "Oh, money he all gone!" is the usual answer, "Squaw he want so much buy ribbons." An Indian speaks of all things in the masculine gender. He probably never pays you back the dollar, so you have to take it out in mocassins or other things.

It is a bad plan to give presents to Indians, or pay them more than you bargain for, except in rare cases, as they are never satisfied and expect the next person who employs them to do the same. I do not think that gratitude is known amongst them; at the same time they are very hospitable to one another, or to a stranger that comes along. I have had a good meal before now in a red man's camp—at times too when it was most acceptable; as a rule they are perfectly honest. Indians never say "Sir" in the English sense, or prefix a "Mr." or other title to your name, but simply call you by your surname. By the settlers they are generally addressed as "Brother," especially if the man is a stranger.

The red men are naturally a polite race. I have seen an old Indian when I entered his wigwam receive me with the air of an emperor, and hand me a seat in the shape of a box or anything else available with the utmost politeness. There is nothing snobbish or uncouth about the genuine red man—quite the reverse; he is vastly superior to the African negro, and not to be even named with him, or to make use of an Americanism, "The negro could not begin to compare with him." The red man has a great amount of self-respect, and unless drunk rarely makes a fool of himself; he is taciturn, but all observant. The negro, on the other hand, however much he is civilized, is an inordinately vain pompous fool. His laugh is quite enough to stamp his character without further inquiry; he will live on any garbage to enable him to buy Brummagum jewellery and smart clothes. The Indian on the contrary rather inclines to the other extreme, and his money all goes into his inside and not on to his back. A man of this kind, wearing the most disreputable old patched garments, lives far better than an English labourer.

Almost all the Indians of the Maritime provinces, and many of those in other parts of Canada, are of mixed blood, some of them being three parts white ; but a child reared in the wigwams, though more white than Indian, always grows up an Indian in habits and speech. The only white women in the country who marry Indians are the French ; and this they do frequently. The French settlers are a lower order of people than either the British or Germans. They are bad colonists, and in many

parts of the country are as backward in their
agriculture and farm implements as they were
sixty years ago. The Germans, of whom there
are many in Nova Scotia, are a plodding, money-
saving, industrious race,—slow, but sure. The
Irish vary ; some do well, others live as miserably as in their mud cabins in the Emerald Isle.
English settlers do well, but are not so numerous
as the other nationalities. The Scotch almost
always thrive ; and, taken as a whole, are the
best off. The Nashwauk valley, opposite Fredericton, is almost entirely peopled by Scotch-
men, many of them the descendants of old soldiers belonging to the 42nd, which corps, in former times, was stationed several years in New
Brunswick.

The settlers of North America are a most hospitable and kind set of people. Some have very
good farms, and are well off, especially in the
neighbourhood of large towns, rivers or railways.
Those living in the back settlements—as they
are called—away from any river, main-road, or
line of railway, are generally poor. There is not
much actual money made by farming in this
country ; but a man has always plenty to eat,

and sells enough to buy clothes and other things which he does not raise on his farm.

The absence of a good market in many parts of the Maritime provinces, is a drawback, and a farmer has to take what he can get for his produce, which consists chiefly of hay and oats. Wheat is hardly grown at all, the season being too short for its cultivation ; and, some years ago it got all blighted, and since then the people have not attempted to grow wheat in any quantity. In the western states of Canada, where the seasons are longer and the land more cleared, plenty of wheat is grown, and that part of the country altogether is more adapted for all kinds of farming.

Oats have been exported to England from Prince Edward's Island, which is one of the best cultivated and most forward provinces in the way of agriculture. There are regular hedges there, but in all other parts of the country the snake fence almost entirely predominates. These fences are formed by placing cedar, or other poles, at an angle, their ends resting one over the other; their weight keeping the structure in its place. There are several ways of making a fence with poles, without the use of nails. A cedar snake fence will last many years; there are some in the State of Maine said to be nearly one hundred years old.

Now that the western extension line is open, connecting St. John with Bangor in the United States, and traversing in its route the valley of the St. John river, farmers are able to get a good price for their hay and other produce. A good deal of the former is compressed, and sent to a distant market. In old days, farmers got only from thirty to forty cents a bushel for their oats at Fredericton, and were glad to get even that.

The houses of settlers never have any trees round them; of course, in the first instance, the primeval forest has been cleared, but if a few young trees were afterwards planted round the dwellings, they would keep off the cold winds in winter, and add much to the warmth of the habitation, besides forming a pleasant shade in summer. But the people have no idea of planting a tree, nor do they, as a rule, ever have gardens attached to their houses, although vegetables and fruit grow well.

Apple trees are an exception, and orchards are numerous, especially in the Anapolis valley, Nova Scotia, where cider is manufactured, but of poor quality, and it generally becomes sour in the hot weather from want of strength. Nova Scotia is more forward than New Brunswick in the way of settlements, and contains many capital farms, especially in the cider producing valley above-mentioned. The people there are of a singularly rough and ready stamp, and can do anything from building a sled to a boat.

The ship building trade of New Brunswick has much declined of late years, owing to the substitution of iron for wooden ships, particularly for those of large tonnage; a good many small vessels however are still built.

With regard to manufactories, Nova Scotia, from its coal and iron, is destined to become the Staffordshire of the Dominion. There are plenty of minerals, such as iron, lead and copper, in different parts of the country, but Nova Scotia is more rich in such products than any of the other provinces. Fair success is also met with in the gold fields of that province. There is a cotton factory at St. John, New Brunswick, and one has been talked about at Halifax, but nothing has come of it. The great drawback to the establishment of manufactories is the scarcity of capital, and the want of energy with those who have it.

Formerly, all manufactured articles either came from the States, or were imported from England, but excellent steam machinery is now manufactured both at St. John and Halifax. At Pictou there is an iron foundry that executes good work; there is also a manufactory of pottery in the neighbourhood. In all large towns excellent sleighs are made, whilst axes and skates of the best quality are turned out in thousands. Coal, at Pictou, is two dollars per ton at the pit-mouth. The Cape Breton collieries have also a large yield. The coal lies near the surface, and the expense of raising it is comparatively light. The great drawback is the want of a sufficient market. In the country, wood is so cheap and plentiful that coal is rarely used. Vessels bring out steam coal from England, which comes as ballast, and consequently at a low freight. The American market is almost closed against Canada by the high protective duties, which have come in force since the abolition of the reciprocity treaty. In addition to which, the Cape Breton coal, from the volumes of dense black smoke that it emits, is precluded from use in the men-of-war, and most of the coal used by the mail steamers calling at Halifax is from the old country. Under all these circumstances, combined with the high rate of labour, the collieries barely pay at all. The railways are now making use of coal instead of wood, which helps a little; and the coal trade is certainly not retrograding, and ought in the future, together with the iron, to make Nova Scotia a rich province.

CHAPTER XIII.

Canadian rowdies—Defective state of the police—Immunities from
crime—Popularity of the soldiers—Evil of withdrawing the British
troops from the Dominion—Calamities in consequence to the
matrimonial market—Concerning matrimonial tactics in Canada,
and how they are conducted—The confederation scheme reviewed
—Necessity for extended railway communication—Evils of the
truck system—Hardships of the settlers—The Ashburton treaty.

THE lower population of the towns —" boy-hoys "
is the local term, answering to the "lambs" in
certain manufacturing districts in England—are
without exception the most arrant and cowardly
scoundrels in existence. These ruffians, who are
very jealous of the military, go about in gangs,
and often waylay and maltreat an unfortunate
soldier who is alone, and may perhaps have spent
a too convivial evening. They dare not attack
a man unless he is at a great disadvantage. A
soldier of the 22nd was brutally murdered a few

years ago at Fredericton, and the murderer got
off in the most disgraceful manner.

The police are totally useless, and take particular care to keep out of the way in case of a row.
Last year at Halifax a lot of cabmen actually
entered one of the principal hotels one evening,
and assaulted two gentlemen staying there, who
had refused to pay the exorbitant demands of one
of the cab drivers during the day.

There are heaps of lawyers and an enormous
amount of litigation in the country.   The laws
are also favourable for swindlers, the common
dodge being to make over your property to your
brother or wife, get into debt as much as possible,
and then bolt to the States.   There have lately
been several serious defalcations among the
cashiers of banks; the worst of it is, that in such
a case, according to the law of the country, it is
merely a breach of trust, and the thief—which
undoubtedly he is—cannot be criminally proceeded against.   In a case of this sort at Halifax,
the other day, where the cashier had made away
with a large sum, the man was not put into gaol
at all, as a medical man, who was a shareholder
in the bank, attested that it would injure his

health. This kind of thing smacks of general
impunity to villains.

Although, as I have stated, among these low
ruffians, there is a jealousy of the military, it is
entirely confined to that class. The country
farmers are very fond of soldiers; and, when travelling, the fact of your being an officer in her
Majesty's service, increases tenfold the hospitality
that is accorded to every stranger. The trades
people in the towns also fraternize with the military; and with regard to the merchants and
others forming the society of the place, their
hospitality and sociability are so well known, that
it would be superfluous of me to treat of it.

Nor is this trait in the character of the people
across the water confined to British America.
The Americans are on all occasions most hospitable to Englishmen; and British officers, when
travelling in the States, always receive the most
unbounded kindness and civility, more especially
from the officers of the American services. During the southern war many British officers visited
the northern armies, and the cordial reception
they met with was most gratifying. Some officers
in my own regiment, under these circumstances,

were sent about in Government steamers, and on land horses were placed at their disposal. On one occasion the colonel of my regiment, when staying at a frontier town of the States, occupied at that time by an American force for the pur- pose of preventing a threatened Fenian raid, on calling for his hotel bill, was informed that it had been paid, having been included in the expenses attached to the route of the American troops, and charged against the United States government. Can the feelings of our own War Office officials be imagined at such an item appearing in a claim for travelling expenses, to wit, "Feeding and lodging one American officer, &c." !

In the society of British North America people see more of each other than in other countries. The towns are isolated, and no one lives in the country in winter, which is the gay time, with the varied amusements of skating, sleighing and dancing. The British soldier, in fact, is the one visible connecting link between the colony and the mother country. This link has been now' rudely snapped by the withdrawal of British troops from all parts of the Dominion, with the exception of Halifax. This measure has given

14

the most intense dissatisfaction to the colonists, and has created a soreness which will take years to heal. It has given rise to the feeling that England wishes to desert them, and many of the people in consequence talk of annexation. The Canadians naturally, from their intercourse with the United States, have adopted to a great extent the manners, customs, and form of speech of the Americans.

The regiments stationed in North America leave behind hundreds of discharged soldiers. Surely this leaven of English troops must be of some service to the country; added to which their militia could always get drill instructors from the regular army, and the officers were also attached to the different corps for the purposes of drill, &c. At the time of the Trent affair the British troops were entertained at most of the large towns. At St. John, New Brunswick, dinners were given to the men of every regiment that passed through. At that time the loyalty of the country was not to be questioned; but now it has received a severe blow. Two regiments stationed in Lower Canada, one at Quebec and another at Montreal, would have quite satisfied the colonists. But for the sake of this thousand men, which, under the present establishment, is the number of two corps—about the number of Frenchmen the Prussians would polish off in a skirmish before breakfast—all this ill feeling and want of trust has been originated. As regards the expense, rations are much cheaper in Canada than in England, and the barracks are provided in many instances by the colonial government.

The withdrawal of troops from Upper and Lower Canada will cause an unprecedented fall in the matrimonial market of those " sections." The loss of so many bachelors in the shape of the officers of the army will be severely felt. Canada has proved more fatal to celibacy than any other country where troops are stationed, including even England. Let not my readers suppose that the frequent sacrifices at the altar of Hymen are due to the superior attractions and beauty of the Canadian ladies—not that I wish to detract from their charms—for the " Merry maids of England" still bear away the palm! The reason is, the propinquity and opportunity that is afforded where people are congregated in a small space, and where long absence from home often " makes the heart grow fonder," *of some one else.*

A young and not over wise man meets a lady
at the skating rink, who rather takes his fancy;
she seeing at once that an impression is made,
meets him quite half way, often more so. Day
by day, hand in hand, they glide round the icy
circle; invitations to tea at divers houses follow,
where curiously enough they always happen to
meet. The mothers on these occasions appear
to form a sort of secret mutual help society.
The youth alluded to, becomes suddenly a pro-
moter of sleighing parties, and dances; in one he
of course drives the fair one, and at the other
dances with her all night. In the end he is
often secured, as tight as a sable in a dead-fall,
unless he is suddenly ordered away, or goes on
leave. Some commanding officers, when any
officer of their regiment got severely wounded,
sent him away on leave. My own respected
Chief did not follow this plan, or some of us,
who were deaf to the voice of the charmer,
might have hovered near the bait, with the intention of eventually setting many dead-falls,
and shooting sundry animals.

As a general rule, the male members of a
family are entirely ignored in all invitations

given by the officers; this is an understood thing
and quite acquiesced in by the ladies.   But now
a change has come over the spirit of the dream,
and the ladies of Canada will have to be more
civil to the native gentlemen of the country
—those whom formerly they cut at the rink,
asked not to the pic-nic, and threw over in the
ball-room.

It is sad to think that the citadel of Quebec,
where, since the days of Wolf, the British sentry
has paced his monotonous beat, will now know
him no more, and the ancient gateway be handed
over to the charge of perhaps, a solitary " peeler."

With respect to the confederation of the provinces of Upper and Lower Canada, New Brunswick and Nova Scotia, into what is now termed
the Dominion of Canada, there is a good deal to
be said on both sides.   Nova Scotians are still
averse to the new state of things, and particularly at the way in which the measure was
smuggled through the Houses of Parliament,
without an appeal to the country.   Prince Ed-
wards Island and Newfoundland still hold out,
and refuse to join the Dominion.   There was a
decided opinion among the colonists in favour of

confederation of the Maritime provinces, Lower and Upper Canada to form a separate confederation. I am inclined to agree with such a course, which would have given general satisfaction, and paved the way for a further juncture of the whole country. The course that has been pursued is rather a case of trying to run before attempting to walk; at the same time it cannot be denied that the present state of things is better than if the provinces had remained in *statu quo.*

Railroads are now greatly required to open up the country. The Inter-Colonial line between Halifax and Quebec is progressing slowly. Labour is scarce, and the lumberers who earn in reality about twenty-five cents a day in the woods, consider it *infra dig.* to handle the pick and shovel, and will not work on the lines, although the wages are from a dollar a day and upwards, and cash " at that." As soon as this line is finished it ought to increase the importance of Halifax as a sea port. The bad navigation of the St. Lawrence can be avoided, and the colonists will be independent in winter of the American line from Portland, where heavy dues are paid by ships entering the port, and emigrants charged a dollar a head for the privilege of landing. This tax is paid by the steam companies, but of course added to the fare.

These lines have been talked about for years, but the cry always was, they can't pay, who ever expected they could pay as an immediate investment? Did any one suppose the Pacific Railroad would pay? At the same time every man conversant with America is aware that it will tend in future to increase immensely the prosperity and wealth of the country, and is one of the grandest undertakings ever carried out by the Americans. Where was a howling wilderness on the introduction of the "iron horse," becomes a line of thriving settlements—this especially applies to the Dominion, where there are no hostile Indians to interfere with the settlers.

The completion of the line to Quebec, which runs along the north shore of New Brunswick, crossing the Mirimichi, Nepisiguit and Restigouche, will tend to cheapen provisions in those regions, which during the winter, are comparatively isolated; the poor settlers will also be enabled to emancipate themselves from the thraldom of the truck system, which weighs on them heavily. The same flour that could be bought in St. John for six dollars a barrel is there charged at about double the price. The people are paid by a "do bill," as it is termed, on the store, and being kept carefully in the debt of their employer, who is also the storekeeper, are obliged either to submit to these exorbitant charges or accept the alternative, starvation.

The most glaring robbery under the truck system in these out of the way places is in the lumber business. A man goes into the woods in November, and comes out in June; nor does he receive a penny in cash until then. If during the time he is in the woods, and after perhaps he has been working some months, he requires tobacco and clothes, or may be his wife at the settlements a barrel of flour, he is charged the full credit prices for these articles, though he is giving six months credit to his employer for his labour. The result is, that when the settling day arrives, he perhaps receives only a few dollars in cash, and has sometimes difficulty in getting it.

I have often heard the lumberers complain of this state of things, and always told them that the remedy was in their own hands—they should combine together, and when the stream driving commenced, strike *en masse* for cash and ready money payments, or ready money prices, provided the sums did not exceed the wages they were entitled to. By this means they would have their employers on the hip, as on the water falling the lumber would be "hung up," and could not possibly be got down till the following spring.

At Bathurst the chief agent of a large lumbering firm was a particularly hard man to deal with, a Methodistical psalm-singing Scotchman, who attended meeting three times on Sunday, but whose treatment and language to his workmen the rest of the week was not angelic. A man with a large bell went round the village before daylight to awaken the workmen and prevent them being a moment late at the saw mill. Pleasant for the inhabitants! I wonder no one ever varied the amusement by practising with the big drum or other noisy instrument under the agent's windows at a still earlier hour!

People have no conception how in an out of the way place of this kind the wretched settlers are completely under the thumb of the more wealthy storekeeper. Talk of the trodden down British

workman, indeed! and of the bloated aristocracy!
The British workman at any rate is paid in coin
of the realm, and not in rancid pork, or clothes
the principal ingredient of which is shoddy.

It sometimes happens that men of straw—of
course not established firms—after selling their
lumber "skedaddle" to the States without paying
the lumberers. I once met an Indian who had
been treated in this fashion, and who related his
story thus, " Me lumber all winter, Boss no pay,
go off States, one pair of pants that all I got."

At the present time but little money is made
in the lumber trade, except by people of large
capital. The poor settlers are obliged to buy
their supplies at long credit prices, which are so
high, that after the sale of the lumber, they are
often in debt.

Reciprocity with the States would be an im-
mense advantage. The Americans are aware of
this, and hold it over the Canadians *in terrorem.*
This treaty was abolished at the time of the
Southern war, and after the affair of the St.
Alban's raiders, when thirty Confederates went
over from Canada and robbed a bank in the
United States. The men were tried in Canada

and acquitted, but the money was eventually repaid by the Canadian government, who acted most honourably in the transaction. As much cannot be said of the Americans, who have twice winked at and allowed a Fenian raid to be made on Canada, when hundreds of Fenians had congregated on American territory with the avowed and well known purpose of crossing the border; not to mention the lionizing of the lately released Fenian convicts.

What the upshot of the present fishery question will be, remains to be proved. The Americans considered themselves agrieved because former privileges were annulled consequent on their refusal to re-establish the reciprocity treaty, and they have also threatened to stop goods being forwarded in bond from Portland to Quebec; such being the case, the sooner the inter-colonial line is finished the better. I have no doubt that in any diplomatic business with the Americans we shall come out second best, as was so pre-eminently the case in the disgraceful Ashburton treaty, when in defining the boundary the Americans managed to extend the State of Maine into New Brunswick in the form of a wedge, cutting off the heads of the St. John river, with permission for all lumber cut in the State of Maine to be driven to the sea free of duty. On the other hand lumber cut in New Brunswick pays an export duty.

It has been said that Lord Ashburton—then Mr. Baring—erred in this matter from gross ignorance; however, never did public servant, entrusted with an important mission, fail more disgracefully in carrying it out to the interests of his country. Fortunate for him that he was not serving either the Russian or the French government; for instead of a peerage, he would probably have had his passage paid to Siberia, or found himself where Cayenne pepper was cheap; and most assuredly he would have merited his reward.

It is astonishing—until very lately—how little was really known by the public of the American colonies, their wants, and the general capabilities of the country. At the time of the Trent affair, articles were written in the papers setting forth the immense difficulties of transporting troops from St. John to Quebec by land. One would have supposed that the route lay through the frozen steeps of an uninhabited country; in fact it was merely a long and cold drive over a good road. As to conveyance, the sleighs and horses were easily procured in the country by the contractors for the job, who made a good thing of it. Large camps were easily knocked up at the different halting places, where fuel and food was provided.

A ludicrous picture appeared at that time in the *Illustrated London News*, of " The Guards' march through Canada; " soldiers in snow shoes —which by the way were most unlike those articles—were depicted toiling over snowy mountains. An Indian dressed, *a la* Cooper's novels, with feathers and paint, appeared as guide. The reality was a line of large sleighs, drawn by two or more horses, in which the men were seated, well clad and smoking their pipes, as comfortable as possible.

The grand culminating point in the North American colonies will be arrived at when the Canadian Pacific line is built, whereby immense tracts of fertile country will be opened up. This cannot be expected to take place for several years.

CHAPTER XIV.

Departure from America for Bermuda —Description of Bermuda—First impressions of St. George's— Sir Charles Napier's apt description— Barrack *versus* convict accommodation—Mortality among British soldiers in Bermuda—Frightful ravages of the yellow fever—Disgraceful condition of the graves—Apathy of the home authorities for the comfort or lives of the soldiers—Instances of their neglect —The new fortifications—Lamentable condition of the island.

IN the spring of 1868 my regiment removed from New Brunswick to the Bermudas, that quarter so dreaded by all troops in North America. Early in the autumn of the same year I found myself one morning on board the West Indian mail, bound for those islands. Wistfully, as we steamed down the magnificent harbour of Halifax, I gazed at the forests, leaving behind the abode of the moose, the cariboo and the beaver, and heading for that of the centipede, cockroach and jigger.* Where,

---

* Jigger—a minute insect that lays its eggs beneath the skin, generally in the feet; and if not carefully eradicated, makes a bad sore.

instead of the soft, musical tone of the Indian, the oral nerves are continually jarred by the harsh, idiotic guffaw of the negro; where the fresh smell of the American pine forests is exchanged for that of the *"bouquet d'Afrique;"* where an invigorating, dry atmosphere is replaced by one hot, damp and depressing. The "Alpha," which was the name of our vessel, was a small and good sea boat, though the food and wines were of the worst quality, and the latter most exorbitant in price. This was in some measure compensated for by the captain, who was one of the best skippers I ever sailed with.

On the fourth morning after leaving Halifax, we anchored in the harbour of St. George's, formerly the chief military station in the Bermudas or Somer's Islands. A short description of the place may not be uninteresting to some of my readers, especially to those among them who are in the army, and whose unlucky star has destined them to be ordered to this pestilential spot.

Bermuda consists of a bunch of rocks of coral formation, numbering over three hundred, and varying in size from a few yards square to fifteen miles long, by a mile and a half broad. The

larger islands are in the form of a horse shoe.
The Bermudas are surrounded for the most part
by a circle of coral reefs, extending some ten
miles to sea. There is but one entrance to the
harbours, and that is long, narrow, and very difficult to navigate by day, and at night totally
impracticable. The first view of the scenery, as
you enter the harbour of St. George's, is pleasing
to the eye, though deceptive as a panorama or
stage scene. What in the distance appears to be
boundless tracts of wooded country, on approach
turn out to be merely narrow strips of coral rock,
thinly covered with earth and scrub. The sea is
beautifully clear, and of a bright green colour;
the land undulating, but in general low, with
stunted cedars growing to the water's edge.

The bombastically-styled city of St. George's,
in reality a moderate sized village, is situated in
a hollow between two small hills, and consists,
for the most part, of a collection of wretched
houses jumbled together. The streets are exceedingly narrow, dirty, and offensively odorife-
rous; where—as Sir Charles Napier so aptly de-
scribes it—"The smell of cedar is overpowered
by that of rum." There are no drains, or other

sanitory arrangements in the place. The barracks
are situated on a hill above the town; the officers'
quarters have long since been condemned, and,
when I was last in them, leaked like sieves.   A
patching will take place, and in a few months
they will probably—judging from former attempts
—be as bad as ever.   The other town in the Bermudas is Hamilton, situated on the largest island
of the group, and distant eleven miles from St.
George's.   It is of more recent date, and superior
to the last-named place in every respect, especially
as regards buildings and site.

At the back of Hamilton, about a mile distant,
are the new hut barracks—a monument of War
Office wisdom. (?)   These huts were planned at
home, and sent out from Woolwich in frame, their
narrow eaves do not afford shade from the sun,
and are quite unadapted for a hot climate.   Even
the old tumble-down baracks of St. George's had
good broad verandahs, though the windows had
to be propped open with sticks for want of sashes.
The hut barracks near Hamilton are placed between the only two swamps to be found in the
islands, and have proved in consequence more
unhealthy than others, although they were sup-

15

posed to be model erections and the site the most
salubrious to be found.   There are barracks at
two other places in Bermuda—the Dockyard and
Boaz Island.   The latter were originally built for
convicts and not for British soldiers; it is not
therefore a matter of surprise, that these barracks
and quarters are the best in the whole station.

In the Island of St. George's there is one thing
that must forcibly attract the attention of a new
comer, and that is the number of graves of
British soldiers scattered about on all sides.
Not only in the cemetery, where of course they
are expected, but in the vicinity of hospitals and
camps.   Graves nameless, and with nothing save
a mound to mark where lies the British soldier,
dragged out of the hospital as soon as yellow
fever had done its worst, and buried like a dog
without a coffin—" unwept, unhonoured and un-
sung "—in any place where the earth was easiest
to dig.

Graves of this description are found in places
now overgrown with bushes.   Asking the cause
of some native, you are told that some building
near was a military hospital at the time of yellow
fever in such a year, and those who died were

buried there. Such is the result of numbers of men being left cooped up on these narrow rocks during an epidemic, to perish miserably, when forty-eight hours sail would take them out of an atmosphere reeking with death and black vomit, —the stains of which to this day are visible on the floors of all the officers' quarters at St. George's—to a latitude where that dread pestilence cannot exist! !

Since the epidemic of 1864 orders have at last been issued that in the event of an outbreak of yellow fever the troops are to be immediately encamped at a distance from the towns; and in the event of more than three deaths, the whole garrison to be removed to Halifax. In 1866 there were three deaths among the artillery at St. George's, but on the troops being immediately removed to a distance and a cordon established round the infected locality, no further mischief ensued.

At that time the military chest and the whole of the Government property at St. George's was handed over to the mayor of the town, who organized a corps of black police to take charge of them; and this continued for two months. It might be supposed that the mayor, who exerted himself most indefatigably on this occasion, received some reward from the Home Government in the shape of a douceur, or at least an ample acknowledgment of his services. Far from it; the War Office merely sent him a very cold letter of thanks, which, considering what he had done for them, naturally disgusted that gentleman.

During the epidemic of 1864, when the troops were encamped at the Ferry Point, three miles from St. George's, the guards were daily marched under a broiling sun into the town, then a hotbed of yellow fever. The men did their duty, and returned to camp, in many instances to die of the disease they had contracted. The band and drums, who remained in camp, lost comparatively few men. It was a pity that on former occasions the troops were not removed; these nameless mounds and terribly long lists of names in the cemetèries would not then tell their fatal tale. Besides the visitations of yellow fever, which on an average occur every seven years, typhoid is always hanging about. My regiment at one time had seventy cases of typhoid in hospital.

As shown by the "Army Medical Report," the mortality among the troops in these islands from 1860—67, was greater than that of any station in the globe where white troops are quartered, with the exception of China.

Much has been done since 1869 in the way of drainage at the St. George's barracks, and the officers' quarters have been enlarged, so as to ensure a draught through them. Formerly they had windows only on one side; and in hot weather the officers, to avoid suffocation, slept in the passages. At the present time the troops are turned into navvies, and are employed on the fortifications, which, when finished, will make the islands a second Gibralter. Some of the newly constructed batteries have iron plates defending the embrasures; these plates are secured by bolts on the inside, the effect of which on a shot striking, will be very much that of a mitrailleuse as regards the gunners behind.

This glaring defect was noticed by a French naval officer a few months ago, whose ship happened to touch at the island. He naively remarked that he would prefer risking the enemy's shot outside, to the bolt's inside. Of course the engineers are quite aware of the faulty construction of these plates; but Bermuda is a long way off, a place where worthless gun-boats are sent, to get them out of sight; where there are no prying eyes of newspaper correspondents likely to bring the matter before the public: so when these defects will be made good it is impossible to say.

Now that the black troops have been removed from Jamaica, it would be a good plan to substitute a black for a white regiment at Bermuda, where the work on which the troops are employed, tends to ruin them as soldiers, and deteriorates them as men. The troops are worked all through the summer and in the heat of the day, principally at the different quarries, blasting and cutting stone. How the men can stand the heat and glare at all, I have often wondered.

Whether it even pays to employ troops, in these days of reductions, at such labour, in such a climate, is a matter of doubt. Convicts are the right men for such work, and Bermuda is admirably adapted for a convict establishment, inasmuch as it is difficult to escape from, and with everything calculated to make life miserable.

The former convict establishment was done away
with, owing to the disgraceful amount of crime
and insubordination among the prisoners; though
why discipline should not be maintained at Bermuda as well as Gibralter, I cannot understand.
One cause of the amount of crime was, that instead of being in seperate cells, the prisoners
were confined in large barrack rooms. The
stories one hears from old warders regarding the
iniquities that went on, are quite appalling.

The white inhabitants of the islands are, for
the most part, a pale, sickly race, without energy
of either body or mind, and well adapted to exist
in the wretched spot where first they saw the
light.   Many of them have never left the
place, and there are people of advanced age
who have never even left the one island on which
they were born.

As regards society, there is nothing worthy of
the name.   Amusements are nil, except boating,
which is expensive and soon becomes monotonous.   Of news, there is but one regular mail a
month, which is looked forward to with eager-
ness as the mail day approaches.   Closely, on
the appointed morning, is the signal station

watched, and as the well known and anxiously expected flag is run up, the cry goes forth " The mail! the mail!" At that moment our feelings must have been somewhat akin to those of the Ten Thousand, when they shouted, " Θαλασσα, ω θαλασσα."

There is now a steamer from New York at irregular intervals; but from her mail bags not being sealed and other unknown causes, the letters so frequently miscarry, that she is not to be depended on.

The products of these islands are principally arrowroot, onions, potatoes, lemons and bananas. The soil is rich, and almost anything will flourish, either tropical or otherwise. Cotton, coffee, indigo and tobacco grow wild; aloes have been also grown to advantage. Formerly the revenues of the island were chiefly paid in tobacco. At the present time Bermuda has met the fate of most places, inhabited by the free negro. The remains of good houses in the country testify to the prosperity of the place in old times, when the negro had to work, which he now takes particular care not to do, although wages are high. The result is that a large portion of the soil is uncultivated and allowed to run waste, from the want of labourers on the part of the white, and idleness on the part of the coloured population.

This miserable place containing only about 8,000 inhabitants, has both an upper and lower house of paid members. The duty on some articles is enormous; on wine it is twenty per cent. *ad valorem*, and this is made purposely to affect the garrison, as the troops do not get any drawback on their wines and liquor, which is the reverse in Canada and most other colonies. Meat is one shilling and three pence per pound, fowls one shilling per pound, with the feathers; everything else is dear in proportion. Ice is often not to be had, so you are sometimes reduced to boiled liquor, with the thermometer at ninety degrees in the shade. No extra allowance is given to the troops; the postage is a shilling, and freights from England by mail enormous. In fact, the few merchants there are, live on the army and navy. A few years ago they even attempted to enforce duty on officers' chargers, when landed in the island.

The climate is damp at all seasons and very hot in summer, especially at night when there is rarely any breeze, and even should there be any wind, it is damp, hot, sticky and not refreshing. All clothes must be hung out and aired when-ever a north wind — which is pretty dry — blows, or they will mildew and rot. On such occasions the officers' quarters present the appearance of a vast old clothes establishment. Of noxious insects and reptiles there are not a few, some of the most loathsome character and winged in addition. Of this kind a species of " Norfolk Howard " is the most abominable; it is not uncommon to find such creatures in your soup. There is a beetle called a hardback, that penetrates everywhere, and will walk about with a full tumbler on its back. Flying cockroaches also swarm, and the white inhabitants have been nicknamed the " Cockroaches," as the natives of Gibralter are called the " Rock scorpions." Musquitoes of course infect the houses at all seasons of the year. There are a few small birds on the island, but none of the parrot tribe. The most common are the cardinal grosbeak (*loxia cardinalis,*) the blue bird (*sylvia sialis*) and ground dove (*columba passerina*). The only thing in the shape of game, are a few quail, originally imported from the States, but rarely met with, and affording no sport.

There are several kinds of sea fish at Bermuda, some beautifully marked. The angel fish is a most lovely specimen and combines all the colours of the rainbow; it resembles in shape a bream with two long yellow and blue streamers. All the fish of the island are indifferent eating, and taste like a pike out of season. There is a species of locust that breaks the otherwise still night by a jarring sound, as if half a dozen men were grinding razors. A curious fact in this place is, that the cocks crow at night from eleven to twelve. Tree coral is found here in all kinds of fantastic shapes, together with some pretty shells. There are no springs in the islands, and rain water is collected in large tanks.

A brother officer, on his passage out, received some curious answers to his inquiries about the islands; an old skipper in reply to his questions, said, that Bermuda was " a very one hoss place." On another occasion a Yankee informed him that if he owned Hades and Bermuda, he would live in Hades and let Bermuda.

CHAPTER XV.

Prepare to leave Bermuda—Overhaul my hunting kit—Determination
not to abandon old friends—Departure from Bermuda—Feelings
of delight at leaving its gloomy shores—Arrival at Halifax—
Revisit Fredericton—Sad change in the old familiar spot—Discharged soldiers—Re-engage Sebattis—Sail for St. John's, Newfoundland.

AFTER spending many weary and monotonous
months in Bermuda—that never sufficiently to
be accursed spot—the arrival of two officers from
England enabled me to take my turn of leave.
Several days elapsed before the return of the
mail steamer from St. Thomas on her way back
to Halifax. I now determined to carry out a
long cherished scheme of an expedition to the
interior of Newfoundland, to the shores of which
on my passage out from England I had cast a
longing eye.

After the manner of Mr. Briggs I began to

get my shooting and fishing tackle in order, to
sort feathers and other fly-making materials, to
cast bullets and make cartridges for gun and
rifle, also to overhaul my hunting kit. Thick
socks, knickerbockers, blanket coat, &c.—which
made me feel quite hot to look at—were brought
to light, more or less damaged by damp and moths.
Among other things was that identical old shooting jacket which I wore on the occasion of the
capture of a big salmon in the Metapedia. How
instantaneously does the whole scene come before
me! How after an hour's play he was cleverly
gaffed by Peter and deposited safely on the rocky
bank! That garment too has been present at
the death of many a cariboo. I wore it also on
that memorable occasion at Napadogan, when
Sebattis called up that big moose, visions of whose
death are conjured up as I gaze on it. Yes, I
will keep that jacket though patched and faded,
for in it lies an enchantment more powerful than
any which resided in the crystal sphere of Cor-
nelius Agrippa, when spiritual visions were dis-
cernible. I remember the words of Ronald of
the Mist, "Barter it neither for the rich garment,
nor for the stone roof, nor for the covered board,

nor for the couch of down;" nor will I hand it
over to my servant who will sell it for the sum
of eighteen pence, which is all he is likely to
extract from the Israelite; I will keep it therefore as a memorial of the past, and wear it yet
once again on the hills of Newfoundland, where
may it prove a talisman of success; and when it
shall be unfit for me to wear it more, I will bestow
it upon some worthy successor of the ancient red
man, who shall carry it again into the depths of
the forest and wear it on the hunting path by
day, and at the camp fire by night, until it is
torn up for gun rags.

Having collected all my tackle and carefully
packed my " pitsnargan " with all necessary requisites, on the 1st of August I steamed out of
the harbour of St. George's, with very different sen-
sations to those with which many months before
I had entered it.   Now I was about to exchange
a land of *ennui* and depression for one where
there is all to please the eye and raise the spirits
to the highest pitch. Now I shall exchange the
warm dirty tank water for the cold spring brook
bubbling beneath the tall fir and verdant birch,
the hot damp atmosphere of Bermuda for the

fresh breezes of North America. Indeed one feels quite another being on passing the gulf stream. After forty-eight hours steaming, the climate has totally changed, instead of wearing the thinnest and lightest of clothes, you are glad to put on a pea jacket, and *vice versa.* On my arrival at Halifax I set about the purchase of two canoes, but was only able to procure one small Micmac of a suitable size for " portaging." I then proceeded to New Brunswick, and paid a visit to Fredericton, where I looked up all my old friends at the Indian camp. My sudden appearance there caused rather a sensation. Poor Noel Lolah I was very sorry to find dying of consumption; he was a good hunter and a keen sportsman. Many a time had we hunted cariboo together, and many a pipe had we smoked by the camp fire.

The barracks at Fredericton were still in the old spot alongside the noble river, but nowhere was to be seen the familiar British soldier. Grass was growing in what used to be the well-kept walk; what was once a smooth lawn, was now ragged and unkempt. A general appearance of dilapidation prevailed. There stood the

billiard-room built by my regiment; I looked
through the broken windows, the ceiling was
fast going to decay, and spiders had taken pos-
session of the walls. There were the seats on
which I had so often sat, where the merry laugh
resounded—now all was still. In the barrack
yard I recognized the identical old barrel formerly the habitation of my faithful spaniel—
Musquash. It gave me quite a fit of the blues
to see the old place so silent and neglected.

In the streets I was accosted by several discharged old soldiers, who, hearing of my arrival,
had come out to see me, right glad to meet an
officer of their regiment and shake him by the
hand. Ye civilians who talk so fluently about
army reform and advocate changes, the adoption
of which would be the destruction of the " regi-
mental system," how little ye know of the bond
between the officer and the old soldier, or of the
affection of both for the old corps !

I was able to purchase a good canoe at
Fredericton, with which I returned to St. John,
and the next day made my way to the camp of
old Sebattis, whose whereabouts I had some difficulty in finding. On approaching his wigwam

I gave a loud and well-known hulloa, which
Sebattis recognised, and coming out, with surprise depicted on his countenance, exclaimed,
" Dashwood, by heavens ! "   I at once engaged
him to accompany me to Newfoundland, and
directed him to join me the same evening at my
hotel.   I also told him to get some rock maple
for paddles and axe handles, as I had been informed that there was none to be had in Newfoundland.   In due time Sebattis made his appearance with a lot of rock maple, and we left
the same evening for Halifax.   There I hired
another Indian named Stephen, and having got
all my supplies, embarked next morning with
two canoes and my two men on board the Newfoundland mail.   On leaving the harbour we
passed close to the Bermudian mail, which like
ourselves was outward bound.   I waved my
hat to my friend the Captain, accompanied by a
triumphant shout.   I was in the right ship
this voyage at any rate.   Speed on, oh Alpha, to
yonder pestilential rocks, this time without my
company !

16

CHAPTER XVI.

First discovery of Newfoundland—Welsh legend—The fate of the aborigines—Their habits and customs—Mode of burial—Their mys-
terious extinction—The settlers in Newfoundland—Their poverty
and extraordinary ignorance—Their bigotry and hospitality—
Government abuses—Concerning some peculiar habits of the
settlers—The fisheries and farming—Mineral wealth of the
country.

In the History of Wales it is written that in
the year 1170, Madoc, son of Owen Gwyneth,
"prepared certain ships with men and munitions
and sought adventures by seas; sailing west and
leaving the coast of Ireland, so far north, that
he came unto a land unknown, where he saw
many strange things." It is supposed by some
that Newfoundland, by others that the West
Indies, was the unknown land discovered by
Madoc.

It is stated in Campbell's Lives of the Admirals, that the first authentic discovery of that Island, was made in the year 1497, by John Cabbot, a Venetian, who settled at Bristol, and was granted a patent by the King of England to discover unknown lands and conquer and settle them. The island was called by Cabbot Baccaloa, the Indian word meaning fish, from the abundance of fish upon that coast.

The aborigines of the country were the Bœ-othic or Red Indians, so called from their habit of painting their skins with ochre. A mystery hangs over the fate of these people, who for many years have been extinct on the island. All attempts to civilize them failed. They committed depredations on the property of the early settlers whenever an opportunity offered, stealing more especially knives and axes or any-thing iron. The settlers, on the other hand, shot them down like dogs whenever they were seen.

The Red Indians lived, for the most part, on the flesh of the cariboo. These animals they killed in large numbers every autumn, during their annual migration, the following being the means adopted:—Strong fences were built by the Indians, sometimes miles in length, so situated as to oblige the deer to cross the lakes at particular points.   While swimming across they were easily overtaken in canoes and speared. The flesh was then dried, the skins manufactured into clothes and mocassins, sewn with thread made of the back sinews of the animals.

M'Cormack, one of the first travellers who penetrated into the interior of the country, relates many interesting facts regarding the habits and customs of these people.   The same writer mentions that their dwellings, although conical and the frame made of poles covered with skins or bark similar to an ordinary Indian wigwam, had each a circular cavity dug in the earth and lined with moss or boughs.   From this peculiarity it has been conjectured that the natives slept in a sitting position.   But I think the most reasonable hypothesis is, that the cavity was formed for the sake of warmth.

The spear heads and axes of these people were made of flint and their cooking utensils of birch bark.   Regarding their burial places, M'Cormack relates that they were constructed according to the rank of the persons entombed.

The body was wrapped in birch bark and with the property of the deceased, placed on a scaffold about four feet high. Sometimes the body was bent, folded in birch bark and enclosed in a sort of strong box made of square posts. The most common mode of burial, however, was that of placing the body in a wrapper of birch bark and covering it with a pile of stones.

In 1810 Sir Thomas Duckworth published a proclamation for the protection of the Red Indians, and soon afterwards Lieutenant Buchan of the Royal Navy, was sent to the river of Exploits, with orders to winter there, and if possible to effect a communication with the natives. The expedition under this officer proceeded up the river Exploits in the winter, and after many difficulties, he met with a camp of Indians near Red Indian pond. Having made them presents and otherwise conciliated them, two of the Indians were induced to return with the party to the settlement, a couple of mariners having volunteered to remain as hostages. During the return of the expedition to the coast, the two Indians got frightened, and effected their escape. Lieutenant Buchan returned at once to the Indian camp, and there found his mariners had been murdered and the natives had decamped for parts unknown.

In 1817 a woman was captured by some trappers, but she died in the course of a year. Nothing more was seen or heard of these people until 1823, when a party were seen near Notre Dame Bay, by some trappers, who shot a man and took a woman prisoner. This female was taken to St. John's, where she lived several years.

In the year 1827 M'Cormack undertook an expedition in search of the Red Indians; but after wandering about the interior of the island for some time, and finding many old encampments, he returned without success. It is generally supposed that the remains of this peculiar people must have passed over to Labrador, somewhere about the year 1825, though at the present time there is no tribe of Indians on the mainland, who from their appearance or habits might be supposed to be their descendants.

The island of Newfoundland is the least settled of any of the Maritime provinces of Canada. With the exception of the neighbourhood of St. John's and Harbour Grace, there is scarcely

a road in any part of the country. The sole
means of communication is by sea, and that only
during the summer months. At that season the
traffic is carried on by coasting schooners, with
the exception of one steamer, which makes two
or three trips during the year. In winter all the
bays are frozen or rendered unnavigable by floating ice. The population, which is thinly scattered all along the coast, live almost entirely by
fishing, principally the cod fisheries, and are for
the most part, an exceedingly poor and improvi-
dent people. They do not take to farming, and
if the fisheries turn out bad, many of the people
are nearly starved during the winter. The
truck system is universal in this country, and
the fisherman, after paying all expenses of outfit
and provisions for the season, has but little left
in cash.

Many of the inhabitants of the more remote
bays have never left the neighbourhood in which
they were born; the ignorance of some of these
people is hardly to be credited. A short time
since on the discovery of a mine on the east coast
of the island, some horses and cows were transported thither; a horse happening to stray away

was shot by a settler as an unknown wild animal.
In the course of skinning the beast the man
discovered its iron shoes ; this appeared to him
such an extraordinary occurrence that he attri-
buted it to a supernatural agency—as ignorant
people are liable to do things they do not understand—and departed quickly from the spot, leaving the horse where he had killed it. The people at
this remote place, on first seeing a cow, exclaimed,
" Here comes an animal with powder horns
growing on its head !" They had used cow horns
for that purpose all their lives, without knowing
their origin. In another instance two men had
a dispute over a cow, as to whether it was
not a horse. These people, it must be borne in
mind, are all free and independent electors. Most
of the inhabitants of Newfoundland are Catholics,
and at St. John's religious feeling runs high.
It would be difficult to get a Roman Catholic
jury to convict a Catholic of any crime against
a Protestant. A notable instance of this, and a
most atrocious failure of justice, occurred some
few years ago, when a Catholic jury refused to
convict a Catholic of the murder of a Protestant,
though the evidence was as clear as the sun at
noon day.

The Newfoundlanders are most abominable wreckers. A ship getting ashore on the island is very likely to be gutted by the surrounding inhabitants, unless there is sufficient force to repel them. If caught, they are often treated with leniency by the laws of the land. But, though lawless, the people of the country are most hospitable. The poorest man would readily give you of his best to eat, and be insulted if you offered payment. Until lately there were many glaring government abuses in force, amongst which was a grant of money voted annually to be spent in meal and molasses for the relief of the poor. This money was handed over to the different members of Parliament to be distributed in their districts. The only member of the government who had not a share, was awarded the contract to supply the meal and molasses. There is a story of one honourable (?) member who paid off his bad debts in a certain district with pauper rations. Those people in his debt, entitled to relief, received none, their debts being cancelled instead.

Another monstrous abuse was the money voted for roads, which likewise was handed over to the members for distribution among various settlers; no account was kept of the expenditure of this money. A settler in one of the bays, to whom money had been given to lay out on roads, being asked as to the roads he had built, pointed to one from his own door to the sea with a wharf at the end of it; on being remonstrated with, the man replied that the road was public, and anyone might make use of it. These abuses have been abolished by the government now in office.

The system of coinage in Newfoundland is most puzzling, the currency shilling is here slightly different in value to that of the Dominion currency—value, tenpence. Even in the Dominion the value of the dollar varies in different provinces. In Nova Scotia the dollar is worth four shillings sterling, in New Brunswick four shillings and twopence. In the latter province a sovereign in gold is worth three pence over the twenty shillings. In Nova Scotia no such premium is allowed. In reality, currency money is of no use to the country, as all the banks, public offices and large mercantile houses use the American system of dollars and cents, which is far more simple and easy to calculate.

The Newfoundlanders have so far refused to join the new Dominion. I think that they are just as well out of it, as they have nothing to gain by the extension of railways on the main land. At the same time it is ridiculous that they have not free trade with other parts of British North America. The Canadians are inclined to put the screw on the non-Confederating colonies in the shape of heavy duties on their produce, in order to compel them to join the Confederation. As has before been mentioned a Maritime Confederation would have been the best course to have commenced with.

The troops have now been entirely removed from Newfoundland. As the roughs of St. John's, who congregate there at the end of the fishing season, are a most lawless set, I should not be surprised to hear any day that they had looted the town. They attempted to do so once, but were kept in order by the troops, who were compelled to fire on the rioters.

The settlers of Newfoundland, in common with all others of North America, are most fastidious as regards the portions of an animal they will eat. No one will touch either the heart or other

part of the insides of an animal; pigs' and lambs'
fry are thrown away, and sweetbreads and giblets
are cast aside. There was a fine at St. John,
New Brunswick, for bringing geese to market
with the giblets in them. Pigs' feet, lambs' head,
and ox tails are also discarded—a useless waste
of good food. Happening to see an Irish settler
one day throwing away an ox·tail, I remarked,
"You are leaving one of the best parts of the
beast." He looked up with a face, as much as
to say "Don't gammon me," and replied, "Ah,
it would take a mighty deal of sauce before a
man could eat that." I told the idiot he deserved
to starve until he had eaten it, and that many an
Englishman, I for one, would be glad of it. Not
that you can convince these people of their
wasteful folly; they are much too obstinate.
The tail of an ox is often thrown in with the
hide, which is sold by weight.

One great drawback to the prosperity of Newfoundland and to the settlement of the country,
is that in accordance with the treaty of Utrecht,
the French have practically the exclusive right
of the sea fisheries to the north of Cape John,
the best half of the island. The Newfound-

landers therefore are compelled to make a voyage of three or four hundred miles to Labrador. The French shore, as it is called, is hardly inhabited at all. The French, not being allowed to build permanent dwellings or settle, return to France after the fishing season, leaving their boats and stages for drying fish in charge of some few New·foundlanders. There have been several *fracas* lately between the French and the colonial fisher-men. Large fortunes are made by St. John's merchants in the fishery trade. The cod fish are salted and dried, the best quality being sent to Spain and Portugal, the next best to the West Indies, and the worst to England.

The common seal (*phoca vitullina*) is very plentiful on the coasts of Newfoundland early in the year. The seal fishery, which for the short time it lasts is more valuable than the cod, commences about the 1st of March, and formerly was carried on by means of sailing vessels, generally large schooners. These often get wind-bound and enclosed in the ice, where they are sometimes shut up many weeks, and return to port without taking a seal. At the present time the most successful ventures are made by steamers;

several of which leave St. John's every year carrying a large number of men, who receive a portion of the profits at the end of the voyage, a man sometimes earning as much as twenty or thirty pounds as his share.

In the first trip of the season, the young seals, or pups, as they are termed, are almost exclu-sively taken. During the first stages of the growth of the pups it is necessary that they should pass long periods of repose out of the water. They are thus met with in vast quan-tities on the floating fields of ice, a small floating piece of which is called a pan. On falling in with a number of young seals, the men distri-bute themselves over the ice and kill them by a blow on the nose, with a kind of wooden club carried for the purpose. They are then skinned, the fat removed and the carcasses thrown away.

In the second trip made by the sealers later in the spring, the old seals are killed. These are too wary to be approached and knocked on the head, so have to be shot, for which purpose the Newfoundlanders use long and heavy guns, made before the year *one*—if it were possible,—into which they cram an enormous charge of the worst of powder, with slugs or buck shot. It almost knocks a man down to fire off one of these engines, and his arms are black and blue after a day's sealing.

The sealers are atrocious marksmen, and a good shot, with a handy rifle, could kill twice as many seals as one of the natives. They despise a fowling piece of ordinary size. A settler who once inspected my twelve-bore gun, remarked, "I guess it won't kill anything bigger than a mouse." My charge of powder they also laughed at, as ridiculously small; four or five fingers, including shot, in a large bore, being considered a proper charge. A large seal skin at St. John's fetches about a dollar. I can fancy a lady reader exclaiming, "Oh, what a place to get sealskin jackets!" But these are the hair seals; the fur species, which are made into jackets, inhabit the South Seas, as many of my readers are doubtless aware.

The climate of Newfoundland is ill-adapted for farming, owing to the coldness and especially the shortness of the summer. There is an immense fall of snow every winter, and though the cold at that season is not so intense as in Canada,

the weather is more boisterous and unpleasant.
In summer, the temperature is lower than on
the mainland, and everything is, at least, a fortnight later. I remarked this particularly in the
different berries, of which there are great quantities everywhere. Raspberries, here, are at their
height at a time when they would have been
all over in Canada; the same with strawberries
and blueberries. There are no settlements away
from the coast, except near St. John's and Harbour Grace, and very little attempt at farming
anywhere.

The richness of the country, exclusive of the
fisheries, consists in its minerals, which are just
commencing to be opened up. There are two
valuable copper mines now worked on the east
coast, where nickel is also found, and there are
many others, no doubt, to be discovered in the
country. I noticed several indications of copper
at different places; traces of lead and silver have
been met with, besides iron in many localities.
There is coal in the vicinity of Grand Pond, but
at too great a distance from the sea to pay for
working.

CHAPTER XVII.

Arrive at St. John's, Newfoundland—Start with a brother officer on a
hunting expedition—A respectable Indian—Salmon fishing in
Newfoundland—Difficulties and mishaps encountered during our
expedition—Annoyance from the mosquitoes—Appearance of the
country—Singular absence of hard wood—Animals not found in
the island—Magnificence of the lake scenery—Destruction and
ultimate extinction of the cariboo—A hint for the Newfoundland
Government—Old red Indian remains—Little red Indian pond.

I ARRIVED at St. John's, Newfoundland, with my
men and canoes, three days subsequent to my
departure from Halifax. Meeting there an artillery officer named Bowen, who was on the
point of setting out on a hunting expedition, we
arranged to join our forces, and an excellent companion he proved. Having hired a schooner we
embarked with all our paraphernalia, and after
three days sail were dropped at the entrance of
a large bay, some three hundred miles along the
east coast, which all the way was exceedingly

17

bold and rocky, the water in many places being deep enough close to land to float a good sized vessel. Lighthouses are very scarce in these regions, and some of the schooners returning from the Labrador fisheries are wrecked every year. The water is too deep at any distance from the land to take soundings, which adds very much to the danger of navigation, especially in the fogs which are so prevalent during the summer months.

Leaving our schooner, we managed through the kindness of a gentleman of the name of Gill, who was connected with some mines, to procure a whale boat; into this we packed our traps and set sail, towing our two canoes, in which were seated Sebattis and Stephen, the latter in a great fright, as the sea was rather rough.

After two days coasting we arrived at the head of the bay. On our way thither we met Mr. M‘Kay, the chief owner of a copper mine on the coast, who was returning in his yacht from a fishing expedition. This gentleman most kindly lent us a light skiff he had with him, and offered us every assistance in his power. We camped near the mouth of a river that flowed into the head of the bay There were but aree families

of Indians in the whole neighbourhood, from one
of which we hired a man of the name of Joe, who
proved a capital hunter and well understood all
the secrets of wood-craft, but a more scheming,
avaricious rascal I never met with among the
camps of the red skins.   His exorbitant demands
were caused to a certain extent by a party of
English with more money than discretion, who
some years ago had hired this man, paying the
most ridiculous prices for everything, and throwing their money about in all directions.   As I
have before stated an Indian invariably expects
every man to pay him and give him as much as
another person has done before, and no matter
how much he may have been overpaid, he is
never really satisfied or thankful for anything.

We eventually made a bargain with Joe,
promising him one of my canoes, on which he
had set his heart, if we had good sport.   In one
respect he differed from any other Indian I ever
knew—in that he hoarded up his money like the
veriest Jew, was well off, and owned a good
house and barn.   His go-to-meeting clothes were
of a high order of respectability, and he wore a
silver watch and chain.   It was surprising to

see the Indians in such an out-of-the-way place
so well off. This is accounted for mainly by the
fact that the fire-water of the pale faces is scarce,
and difficult to procure in these regions. Fur is
plentiful, whilst hunters are few, and those there
are thoroughly understand the business of trapping, and follow it up persistently. All the
Indians in Newfoundland are of the Micmac
tribe, and came originally from Cape Breton.
The entire number is very limited indeed, and
the majority of them do not follow up hunting,
but live by fishing.

I killed a few small salmon and any number of
sea trout in the river, at the mouth of which we
were camped. The latter abound in all the
streams of the island, but the former, though
found in many of the rivers, are but small in
size, rarely weighing above six or seven pounds.
I was told by a gentleman who had been years
on a government survey of the island, and a
good sportsman to boot—that he had never killed
a salmon in any part of the country weighing
over seven pounds. The practice pursued by the
settlers of barring the rivers with nets considera-
bly spoils the chance of sport. In some rivers

of Newfoundland the salmon do not rise well to
a fly. In one stream where there were plenty
of peal, they would not take at all, although I
tried on several occasions with all kinds of flies.

There are brown trout in the rivers, of the
same species as in other parts of North America,
but not so numerous, and in the lakes I never
caught or saw a trout that weighed more than a
few ounces. This was the result of many trials
in different parts of the island.

In the course of a few days Sebattis having
manufactured some excellent paddles and axe
handles out of the rock maple I had brought
from New Brunswick, we set out on our journey
up the river, Sebattis and myself in the Milicite
canoe, Stephen in the small Micmac, Bowen and
Joe occupying the skiff. For the first few days
the ascent was not difficult, as the river though
rapid in places was not difficult to pole, and
the water was sufficiently deep. On the fourth
evening we arrived at a chain of lakes and
camped at the outlet; there I caught some nice
brown trout of about a pound to a pound and a
half in weight. The next day our troubles began,
for the river divided and became of course much

narrower. We commenced the ascent of the
left hand branch, and as it came on to rain
before we had gone far, we camped in the hopes
of a rise of water; but the fall of rain proving
but slight, we were disappointed. On our departure the next morning the river had only risen
one inch, and was so low and the bottom so
studded with rocks that we had to wade and tow
our canoes carefully along, lifting them over
some places. In other parts of the river we were
obliged to dig channels in the gravel with our
paddles; for birch bark will not stand dragging
on stones, a canoe being easily cut through by
the sharp point of a rock.

The mosquitoes and black flies were here more
venemous in their bites, and ferocious in their
attacks than any I had met with in America.
Joe informed me that early in the summer the
Indians were obliged to have a slow fire placed
in the bows of their canoes when on the rivers
to keep off the flies. They are more especially
aggravating to a man poling a canoe, as he cannot well knock them off, both his hands being
occupied. On one occasion I was so bitten whilst
getting up a nasty rapid that I jumped out of

Poling up to the Hunting Ground. Newfoundland.

the canoe; I had no tar and lard, as I thought it would not be necessary so late in the year, as would have been the case in New Brunswick.

We continued our course up stream for three days, our progress, from the increasing shallowness of the water, becoming slower and more laborious as we advanced. On the morning of the fourth day it came on to rain heavily, but we pushed on, and at the bottom of a very steep rapid, Stephen lost his balance and fell backwards into the water, upsetting the canoe at the same time. My first intimation of his mishap—I was in the bow—was being pitched headlong into the river. On rising to the surface my first thought was the guns, the flour! I swam to the canoe which had partially righted and got it ashore. Nothing fortunately had fallen out, as the baggage was securely packed and covered with waterproof. The wet had only penetrated the flour about the eighth of an inch, so not much harm was done. Our companions who had witnessed our upset greeted us with roars of laughter; Stephen was not much accustomed to canoes, and could not pole the right hand side, which is usual. This made it doubly hard work for the man in the bow, particularly as regarded keeping the canoe straight.

Towards evening we began to look out for a place to camp in, which having found, we landed our canoes; and turning them bottom upwards, placed all our baggage underneath, as it was still raining in torrents; we then pitched our half-tent and made a big fire. Very tired we all were before this was done, and Stephen began to grumble at the hard work and shewed signs of "caving in," but he only got laughed at by us all. A few bottles of whiskey we had intended to have brought, had been accidentally left behind; for on an occasion of this kind a glass of grog is acceptable. However, we changed our wet things and soon made ourselves thoroughly comfortable, for the water had not penetrated the gunner's bags, wherein were packed spare clothes. I was obliged to take off the locks of my gun and rifle and clean them before turning in, as the wet had penetrated them. The next morning the water had risen a foot, this enabled us to reach by evening the portage to the chain of lakes, which were to form the basis of our hunting operations.

The country through which we had passed, subsequent to our departure from the salt water, was different in its forest growth from Canada. The trees here were smaller and much more scrubby, and the scarcity of hard wood was most conspicuous. The few hard wood trees observable were small, whilst the absence of many well known species was remarkable.

The following trees, common to most parts of North America, are not found in Newfoundland:— the rock maple, cedar, beech, ground ash, moose wood, deer wood and white wood. Yellow and black birch also were not to be seen, though Joe told me there were some few on the western shores of the island.

I noticed several shrubs that did not grow in Canada, but could not find out their proper names, Joe only knowing them by their Indian appellations. The want of the rock maple in Newfoundland is severely felt. It is one of the most useful woods that grows in the forests; the grain is close, and it is exceedingly tough and well adapted for all the uses to which oak and ash are put in England. There are not any oaks in Newfoundland, and but few in the Maritime provinces of Canada. I had, therefore, cause to be thankful for the information that induced me to bring rock maple from New Brunswick. The hard wood that grows in the island is principally white birch and a few small white maples. The trees of the former kind are not big enough to furnish bark for a canoe, hence Joe's anxiety to get one of those I had imported. Poplars are common, but this tree is useless as timber, and for fire wood is the worst that can be found.

The animals that do not inhabit Newfoundland, and which are common to many parts of North America, are:—the moose, red deer, fisher, mink, lynx, ground hog, porcupine, and racoon. Frogs and snakes do not exist. Of birds, neither the wood duck, Canada grouse, ruffled grouse, willow grouse, or woodcock are found. The cariboo is the only species of deer inhabiting the island. It differs somewhat from the animal of the mainland in size and colour, being larger and of a lighter shade. Sometimes the old stags and does are quite white and once I saw a doe of a beautiful cream colour. The horns also are larger and generally curled forwards. The peculiarity of shape is attributable to the openness of

the country.   Cariboo inhabiting thick woods
generally have their antlers straighter than those
living in more open ground.   The superior size
is, no doubt, due to the quality and abundance
of the food in the shape of white moss, which is
more general and of greater luxuriance than
anywhere in Canada.   The deer migrate annually, moving south in the autumn and returning north in the spring.

But to continue—It took us several days to
portage our canoes and other gear, to the uppermost of the chain of lakes, previously mentioned.
These extend for fifty miles, and are the head
waters of a large river flowing into the sea on the
west coast.   On the shore of the uppermost lake
we built a double bark camp and in it stored all
our provisions.   We had some difficulty in getting sufficient bark for the purpose and were
obliged to go a long distance to procure it, some
of the bark was obtained from the vicinity of a
lake twenty miles below our camp.

The scenery here was very beautiful and far
more wild than in any part of North America I had
ever seen. The lakes lay for the most part between
high hills, which descended with a steep slope

to the water's edge and were covered with primeval forest. In the distance could be seen high
mountains, with tops devoid of woods, rising up
from among the forests, in which were conspicuous some splendid pines towering above all the
other trees. One mountain was of a peculiar
sugar-loaf shape, and flat at the top. This, Joe
informed me, was a look-out place of the old
Red Indians. On asking him if he had ever
seen a Red Indian, he replied in the negative;
but that his father had seen their tracks, though
never the men themselves; and, added he, " Red
Indian wild as a deer, he run when he hear
gun."

We had seen several signs of cariboo on our
way up the river, and a few tracks were visible
on the shores of the lake. Bowen and myself
now determined to separate. One of us proceeding to a lake, some thirty miles below which,
according to Joe's account, was the most likely
neighbourhood for sport. I, however, had sus-
picions he was deceiving us; so we drew lots,
and it fell to myself to go thither. The following morning I accordingly left with Joe and
Stephen, taking two canoes. Having paddled

through a series of long lakes, connected by short streams, towards sundown we reached a large lake or "pond," as they are termed by the natives, fifteen miles long and five broad.

Hitherto the shores of the lakes had been more or less rocky, and the woods grew almost to the water's edge, but in this "pond" the beach, which extended about sixty yards from the water to the forest, was formed of the finest white sand. In vain I swept the shores with my glasses for the sight of a deer; a few loons, sailing about and uttering their peculiar weird-like cry, were the only living creatures in sight. We crossed the lake and took up our quarters in an old Indian wigwam, built by hunters.

There was something exceedingly fascinating in such a canoe journey as we had made that day, far away from civilization or the abode of man, where the view varied at every turn, independent of the sport which at any moment might be met with in the shape of deer. The panoramic effects of such a voyage are very beautiful, the changes are not too rapid to mar the completeness of each picture, and the succession of scenic elements falls harmoniously and softly

on eye and mind, allowing them quietly to im-
bibe the beauty, the blending of light and shade,
of pristine nature and her scenes.

In this neighbourhood the land was low,—
large wet barrens, interspersed with lakes and
patches of woods, extending for miles on both
sides the stream. We hunted here far and near
for eight days and saw but one solitary cariboo,
at which I did not get a shot. Joe informed
me that formerly there were many deer in this
vicinity. But of late years the cariboo have de-
creased most lamentably in Newfoundland, from
the slaughter that takes place in winter by the
settlers, at the southermost end of the island,
and I fear in a few years these animals will be
almost extinct. Numbers also have been killed
by the employes on the Atlantic telegraph line.
In the spring when returning to the north, and
when the does are heavy with young, they are
intercepted in certain places at rivers and lakes
chased in skiffs and canoes and killed by scores,
both with the gun, axe and spear.

The slaughter that takes place in the winter
is the most destructive. At that season the
deer congregate in large herds of fifty to a hun-

dred.   Such a herd being discovered in a plain,
an army of pot hunters, armed with sealing
guns, issue forth and surround the deer.   The
herd being fired at, rush towards one side of the
plain, where they are met by a murderous dis-
charge of slugs or buck shot, fired indiscrimi-
nately into their midst.   The same reception
meets them on every side, they get confused and
know not whither to fly; by this means they
are almost exterminated, and of those that escape, many are wounded.   We afterwards killed
several deer with buck shot in them.   I do not
believe at the present time, there is one animal
for fifty there were ten years ago.

I began to get rather disheartened at my
want of success; we were also badly in want of
meat, and had it not been for some beavers we
had trapped and some shell drake flappers I had
shot, we should have been on very short com-
mons indeed.   I had heard so much about the
number of deer and wild fowl that I had brought
a limited supply of pork.   With the exception
of some shell drakes, we had seen but one black
duck and a diver.   The latter I shot, after
creeping several hundred yards, but it proved

18

so tough and strong as to be almost uneatable. So much for the swarms of wild fowl of which we had been told! There were not any grouse on the low lands, nor could I succeed in killing trout in the lakes.

We made an expedition one day to Grand pond, ten miles distant, where there were large barrens, but they proved devoid of cariboo. This lake is the largest in the island and forms a magnificent expanse of water, fifty miles long, with an island in it of twenty miles in length. Traces of coal were visible near the shores of this lake. I now determined to return to the uppermost lake, and on reaching our head quarters I was glad to find my friend Bowen had shot a fat barren doe, which was most acceptable. The deer here, also, were scarce.

The next day I shot a young stag as it landed from the lake, and we caught a fawn swimming by paddling up to, and then lassoing him. He was a jolly little fellow and I should have much liked to have brought him home, as he would have easily been tamed, but he escaped during the night. He ought properly to have been confined in a pen, constructed by driving stakes into the ground and lashing others to them at right angles; he was only tied up, so he managed to slip out of the rope.

How I wished that there were moose in New-foundland! What a place it would be to call on the lakes by our camp. As the moose are now becoming so scarce on the mainland, it would be an excellent plan and one worthy of the consideration of the Newfoundland Govern-ment, to turn up moose in the island. They would not migrate like the cariboo, but remain in the depths of the forest, far out of the reach of the settlers living on the coast. In a few years they would become numerous, and there is plenty of good feeding ground in the woody parts of the island.

We now came to the conclusion that our best plan was to try the high lands, which were dis-tant about twenty miles. Taking a quantity of dried venison, and enough provisions of other kinds to last a fortnight, we lugged them, together with a canoe, to a lake six miles from our camp. This lake was five miles across, and is called Little Red Indian pond. Having crossed it in two trips, we camped on the opposite shore.

In setting a line of traps in the woods near
the margin of this lake, we came across several
traces of the old Red Indians. The places
where their camps stood were clearly to be distinguished, as was also the circular cavity dug
in the earth round the fire place, as described by
M'Cormack. Close to the former site of one old
camp was a large pine, which had evidently in
former years, been chopped by a stone axe or
other blunt instrument. I also picked up a flint
spear head. Leaving our canoe at Red Indian
pond, we set out with the remainder of our luggage to the hills, distant ten miles. A very
hard and tedious day we had; our loads were
heavy, and the way which was steep, lay in
some places through thick woods. At length
near sundown we got to the end of our journey
and camped in a small patch of woods. This
part of the country was more or less open for
miles, undulating and studded here and there
with scrubby spruce and tamarac, and in some
places, with large granite boulders. The higher
ridges were dry and in many spots carpeted
with a luxuriant growth of white moss. In the
lower lands there were marshes, lakes and

brooks. Several kinds of cranberries were plentiful everywhere. Flocks of wild geese soared over head, and packs of the Newfoundland grouse were frequently met with in the open places. These birds, misnamed ptarmigan by the settlers, are apparently the same species as the Norwegian grouse. In summer the tips of the wings only are white, and with the fall they become gradually whiter, until in mid-winter the whole bird is the colour of snow.

These grouse were exceedingly tame and did not afford any sport. It was with difficulty that I could get them up, as when followed and even stoned, they did nothing but run among the scrub. The weather now became wet and boisterous, and getting drenched one night, from the leaking of our half-tent, we all set to work the next day to build a double camp in the island of woods, before mentioned. This was a somewhat difficult matter from the want of bark, or trees favourable for splints. Notwithstanding, we managed to get the latter out of some firs, though with much labour, as the grain was knotty and hard to cleave. At the end of five days' hunting, I succeeded, after a long stalk and

a shot at a hundred and fifty yards, in shooting
a good stag, with fair, though not large horns.
This made up for the bad luck of the previous
day, when I missed fire at a stag, eventually
wounding and losing him. The stag I shot was
in excellent condition, and the fat on his
haunches more than two inches in thickness.
We roasted a haunch on the following Sunday
and it took us nearly all day before it was cooked;
but of all the venison I ever tasted in my life,
that was the most excellent. Though there
were more deer in the hills than in the low
lands, their number was small, and some days
we never even saw one. Very different would
have been the case fifteen years ago, before they
had been destroyed to such an extent.

Our general plan of hunting .was as follows:
We set out at daylight in opposite directions,
with an Indian each; carrying a small kettle,
dried meat, bread, &c. After hunting until
near nine o'clock, I always stopped and had
breakfast, which lasted me through the day.
We tried the plan of a very early breakfast before starting, but at that hour one cannot eat
much, and after four hours walk a second meal

is wanted.   In case I got hungry in the middle
of the day, a bit of dried venison and a pipe sufficed.   Dried venison can be eaten without further cooking, though it is an improvement to
warm it up; with a piece in your pocket and
a pipe and tobacco, you can defy hunger from
morning to evening.   In this manner we tra-
versed daily some thirty miles, reaching camp
frequently after dark, when we talked over the
events of the day, and determined on the course
to be pursued on the morrow.

We shot wild geese on several occasions, but
their flesh was tough.   The cranberries, of which
we collected large quantities, were excellent.
The black flies still continued most troublesome
on a sunny day, though it was now October, and
in Canada they would have been dead long ago.
I began to wonder if they ever died, even at
Christmas.

CHAPTER XVIII.

Cariboo hunting—Shoot a magnificent stag with very large horns—
Exciting chase after a large cariboo—Miss our companions—A
good supper and a miserable night—A visit from Bruin—Return
to headquarters—Beauties of the autumn scenery—Incidents on
our journey home—Genuine hospitality—Arrival at the mines—
Depart for England—Cross the Atlantic in a brig laden with
copper ore—Man overboard—Arrive at Swansea.

NOT to weary my readers with a monotonous
account of our doings from day to day, I will
merely give an account of one good day's sport,
which at the time was especially welcome, as I
had not pulled a trigger for a week. Finding
the deer scarce in the vicinity of our camp, we
agreed to try some country lying the other side
a high ridge, distant nearly twenty miles. We
started at daylight in different directions, arrang-
ing to meet towards sunset at a certain island of
woods, according to Joe's account half a mile

from the opposite side of the ridge, and near to
a large rocky crag which formed a conspicuous
land mark. Stephen was to meet us there with
provisions, and whoever first reached the spot
was to make a smoke as a signal. I had not
gone a mile from camp when Sebattis, who accompanied me, called my attention to an object
about two miles off, which on looking through
my glasses, I at once saw was a cariboo, and of
so white a color that I knew he was almost sure
to be an old stag. In a short time we arrived
at the spot where we had seen the animal, and
followed his tracks a little distance. On rounding
a clump of bushes the beast came in sight; there
he was, a magnificent old white stag, with beautiful horns reaching far back over his withers.
He was leisurely moving along, stopping here
and there for a moment to crop the white moss,
and looking round intently, evidently in search
of does.   Dodging behind the stunted spruce,
I followed him quietly and carefully. After a
stalk of half a mile I got within one hundred
yards of the animal, and as he halted to feed,
fired. Unfortunately just as I pulled the trigger
he made a forward movement, and the ball struck

rather further back than was intended. On
feeling the shot he gave a tremendous bound,
and galloped off. I followed at a run, keeping
out of sight as much as possible. When he
stopped, which he did after a few hundred yards,
I gave him another barrel. This took effect but
low, and he again galloped off, and as he disappeared over a slight rise I gave him a final shot.
An awful apprehension now seized me that he
would escape, together with a sort of sinking
sensation at the thought that I had missed the
biggest cariboo I had ever seen, the great grand-
father of all the deer in the neighbourhood—and
oh, those horns!—breathlessly I ascended the
summit of the hill, anxiously I cast my eyes
ahead, expecting to see the deer careering over
the plain, but to my surprise he was nowhere
in sight. Turning to the Indian, I exclaimed,
"Where is he?" "There, he dying," answered
Sebattis, pointing to a rock fifty yards to our
right, where the noble animal lay breathing his
last gasp. Oh, what a relief, what a moment of
delight never to be forgotten! At last I had
accomplished that for which I had toiled for
weeks, thought of by day and dreamt of by night.

I had killed a cariboo with very large horns. On inspecting the beast he proved to be a stag of more than ordinary size, his height was four feet ten inches at the fore shoulder, his length from nose to tail seven feet five inches, weight about five cwt. His antlers were exceedingly fine, and of a very handsome and unusual growth. He was of great age, and nearly white; his head and neck perfectly so. Joe told me afterwards that he had rarely seen so old or big a stag, " That proper big stag," he called it. The skin was quite soft and furry. My first shot I found had finished him; it took him slantingly, cutting through his lungs. I skinned the head of the cariboo, and returning to our camp for Stephen, who had not left, I sent him back for the skin and meat. Sebattis and I taking the provisions in addition to our blankets, set off for the rendezvous agreed upon.

After a walk of twelve miles we saw a herd of deer four hundred yards from us; thirty does stood in a heap with a large stag following them. A hundred yards behind him two smaller stags were engaged in fighting, butting each other and interlocking their horns. The master stag kept

looking round as if to see that they both kept at a
respectful distance from his harem. We managed
to gain a slight ridge unperceived where I lay
down behind a bush.   The herd was now approaching, the does in front, and I feared at one
time they would come right on to me, but they
turned aside and passed within a hundred yards.
Presently I saw the master stag walking along
with a slow and stately gait. Presenting the
muzzle of my rifle over the bush I fired, away
scampered the does in all directions. I heeded
them not, but followed the big stag who was
rushing madly away.   Loading as I ran, I
stopped and fired another shot as the animal was
crossing a shallow stream. The ball struck him
on the spine, and he fell head over heels into the
water, turning a complete somersault. With a
shout of triumph I rushed up and plunged my
hunting knife into his throat. He was a full
grown stag with very handsome horns, and was
nearly as large as the one I had shot in the
morning, though not so old, or of so white a color.
My first shot had struck him in the neck, and
severed a large vein from which the blood poured
in torrents, so he could not have run much

further. As the day was drawing to a close, we only gutted the deer, pocketed the kidneys and set off at our best pace for the big crag at the top of the ridge.

On reaching this spot I looked in vain for the island of woods described by Joe, or any smoke that might indicate the presence of our companions. For miles nothing was to be seen but granite boulders, scrub and marshes. Here was a dilemma! The sun was setting, and neither Bowen nor Joe had any provisions. We struggled on some distance in the dark among rocks and bushes at the risk of breaking our necks, and at last considered it useless to go any further. A strong wind was blowing from the direction where we expected to meet our companions, so firing signals was of no use. Coming across a large granite boulder we decided upon passing the night there. I collected some sticks and made a fire on the top of the rock as a signal, but it was unanswered. To add to our miseries it came on to rain, fire wood was exceedingly scarce, and the night was so dark that we had difficulty in collecting sufficient fuel to cook our supper, which was by no means a bad one; the bill of fare consisting of cariboo kidneys and grouse, with bread and tea as usual.

We spent a cold, miserable night at this spot, and wished for the break of day long before it appeared. At the earliest dawn we made a good fire and breakfasted off grouse and venison. A thick fog now came on, and we could hardly see fifty yards. Owing to this we were a long time poking about before finding the cariboo I had killed the previous evening. Having skinned him, we set out for home, Sebattis carrying the skin, some meat, &c., and I the head, horns and our blankets, a very awkward and heavy load to carry fourteen miles—our distance from home.

It was dark before we reached our camp—in one place getting into some burnt scrub, our progress was slow, and aggravating. The last half mile we were lighted by an exceedingly bright and beautiful aurora borealis; not a red lurid glare, as generally seen in England, but beautiful pencilled rays of bright silver light darting tremulously over the sky, now faint, and then bursting out suddenly into wondrous beauty.

On reaching camp very tired, and glad to deposit our loads at the door of our habitation, we found Bowen and Joe had arrived a short time before, half starved, having had nothing to eat since the previous morning, nor had they seen a living thing the whole time they were out. Joe had made a mistake as to the locality where we were to have met, hence the cause of our missing our companions. On further comparing notes we discovered that they had passed, during the fog, within a few hundred yards of the spot where Sebattis and myself were enjoying our breakfast.

For several days subsequent to this stroke of luck I did not fall in with any cariboo. Bowen was more fortunate, and on one occasion killed a magnificent stag with larger horns than I ever saw, either before or since, though he was not so old or fine an animal as the big one I had bagged. According to Joe, the horns of Bowen's stag were the largest he had ever seen in his life, they measured three feet nine inches across.

On one occasion when out on a cruise of a couple of days, we found on our return to camp that bruin had called on us and had eaten most of the meat that was hanging up to dry, besides tearing one of our deer skins all to pieces.

The climate now began to set in very cold, especially with an east-wind, and we were obliged to improvise mits out of old stockings. We spent altogether nearly a month in the hills hunting the surrounding country far and near, with but middling success, though we succeeded in shooting a few good stags. The heads of the largest we skinned for stuffing, preserving them in the manner before described in these pages.

On the return to our head quarter camp by the lake, it took us several days to transport thither all our gear, skins, horns, &c. The horns especially were a most troublesome addition to our loads, as they caught continually in the trees and bushes, impeding our progress, which, with eighty pounds on your back, is at all times sufficiently slow. Stephen and myself in crossing Red Indian pond in a canoe heavily laden, got caught in a squall and were nearly swamped. We had to run before it and paddle with all our might to prevent being pooped, as I may call it. At last after very hard work we got all our tackle to headquarters.

On our arrival there we found one of a party

of four officers from Halifax, who were hunting the country forty miles from us. These gentlemen had met with bad luck, having only killed two deer between them in a month. They were also short of provisions, but luckily we had some to spare, including a lot of dried meat. We afterwards sent up half a barrel of flour and a canoe to one of them, directing him to our camp in the hills, whither he proceeded with an Indian and met with some sport. We had dried a large quantity of venison, which the Indians carefully packed to take home for their winter use.

The autumn tints were now in all their glory, and the scenery of the lakes presented quite a different aspect from that we had so much admired on our arrival, if anything it was more beautiful.

The trees in Newfoundland do not turn so suddenly as in other parts of North America, where, as I have before mentioned, three sharp frosts will change the colour of the whole foliage. The cause of this is, that the winter comes on much more gradually in Newfoundland. Up to the beginning of October we had only had two frosts at night, and those not severe, though the

19

days were cold, the wind biting, and the weather
boisterous. There is nothing in the climate of
Newfoundland approaching to what is called the
Indian summer—namely, frosty nights and beau.
tiful warm days late in the autumn.

Our sable line round Red Indian pond proved
a failure, likewise some traps we set near another
lake. There were not any beavers in this locality,
but I saw plenty of houses in the river neaɪ
Grand pond, though " their numerous dome-like
habitations " did not " stud the gliding water,"
as stated by the author of a late sporting work
in the Far West. According to his description,
beavers in the latitudes of which he speaks must
be quite different in their habits to those in other
parts of the world. This at the same time appears
strange, to say the least of it.

Having portaged to the river which we had
ascended on our way up, we found the water high,
and were able to run down without any difficulty.
On arriving at the lakes where the river was
joined by another branch, we halted for a couple
of days and hunted in the neighbourhood with the
hope of getting a deer to take down fresh to the
sea, but we did not see cariboo at this place. On

reaching the coast we put up at Joe's house, a
very swell habitation for an Indian, having a
decent carpeted parlour, with several prints hung
upon the walls.   The difficulty now was how to
get back to St. John's, for we were miles out of
the track of coasting vessels.   Ascertaining that
schooners were in the habit of calling at a copper
mine on the coast, we determined to make our
way thither, so having stowed all our things into
a large boat belonging to Joe, we set sail with
a fair wind.   Putting into a small harbour on
our way, we went to a public-house to get something to eat.   The landlady soon got us a meal
ready, and the master a bottle of rum.   On
tendering payment it was refused, both for the
food and liquor.   We were strangers, they said,
and had come a long journey, so would not take
anything, not that they had any idea who we were.

Bidding these hospitable people good bye, we
set sail and arrived in a couple of days at the
mines.   Here we met with the most unbounded
hospitality and kindness from Mr. McKay, the
owner, whom we had before met in his yacht,
and from Mr. Gill the chief agent.   We put up
at Mr. McKay's house, where we were regaled in

regal style with '34 port and other delicacies—
rather a change in our fare.

Eight hundred men were here employed, and
occupied rows of neat wooden houses. The surrounding country was uninhabited, except by a
few fishermen on the coast. Some of the workmen were Cornishmen, imported for the purpose,
but the Newfoundlanders make good miners.
The best ore is worth £18 per ton, and is
excavated from the side of a hill by driving in
galleries. Nickel is also found in considerable
quantities, and its value is £70 per ton. The
galleries were within one hundred yards of the
sea, so there was no expensive land carriage,
but merely a tramway down to the wharf, alongside which the vessels were able to lie. We
here anxiously awaited the arrival of a schooner
to get on to St. John's, Bowen to join his corps
stationed there, and I *en route* to England, *via*
Halifax. After waiting for more than a fortnight
without any vessel making its appearance, I
determined to embark on board a brig then
loading with copper ore and bound for Swansea.

Bidding good bye to Bowen, old Sebattis, and
all my kind friends at the Mines, I left for that

port. I had never before tried the experiment of crossing the Atlantic in winter in a brig of two hundred and ninety tons burden, carrying a cargo of five hundred and ten tons of copper ore, and I may safely say, that I shall never do so again.

Two days after leaving the land, we met with a severe gale and were obliged to lay to for thirty hours. Our vessel was too much by the stern, and the decks were swept continually by seas coming over the waist. I began to think a berth in the Inman mail would be a desirable change, though after the sad affair of the City of Boston, I might have been worse off. Our fare was not of the best, merely merchant sailor's rations, not that I minded that, but the vessel was so deep that her decks were never dry, even in a heavy swell the sea came rolling over, which was unpleasant. On the sixth day of our voyage the second mate fell overboard and we were unable to recover him, the only two boats being lashed amidships, neither were there any davits by which to lower them, nor any life buoys in the ship. We tried to launch a boat over the side, but she was stove in the attempt. This was another instance of the loss of life due to the rapacious greed of ship owners; for with a life buoy and proper tackle the man might have been recovered. It is high time that legislation stepped in to defend seamen from being exposed to such needless perils, for the want of an outlay of a few pounds. The loss of this poor fellow threw a gloom over us all. The captain, a Welshman, was in a great state, as he was a native of the same village to which the mate belonged. After a voyage of seventeen days we anchored off Swansea, where I was glad to get ashore. My horns, skins and other hunting paraphernalia created considerable astonishment at the different railways, and also on my arrival at the station a few miles from my home—the end of my journey.

Although the shooting I had met with in Newfoundland did not come up to my expectations, from my being fifteen years too late; nor should I be tempted to repeat the visit to that island, as I consider that the expense and waste of time, consequent on the difficulties of locomotion, are not commensurate with the sport to be obtained; at the same time I do not regret having made the trip.   There is always a charm in visiting new fields of operations, of which there are but imperfect accounts, moreover from their being unknown, one is apt to imagine they contain better facilities for sport, than places of which there is a more accurate knowledge.

As far as I can learn one of the best localities at the present time for cariboo, is the region at the heads of the rivers falling into the St. Lawrence, on the coast of the Labrador, where there are high lands and large barrens extending for miles; nor have the deer in that part of the country been killed down to any extent.   I hope some day to build my camp in those latitudes, beneath the towering pine, and the spreading maple; yet again to place the chiploquorgan in the accustomed spot; and as the shades of coming night steal over the forests — whilst the fire burns brightly and the pipe draws freely—discourse of the present, plan for the future, or meditate on the past.

FINIS.